I REMAIN

VOLUME TWO

I REMAIN

The Letters of Lew Welch
&
The Correspondence of His Friends

Volume Two: 1960–1971

Edited by Donald Allen

Grey Fox Press
Bolinas ● California

Frontispiece photograph by Casey Sonnabend, October 1964.

Library of Congress Cataloging in Publication Data

Welch, Lew.
    I remain.

    Includes index.
    CONTENTS: v. 1. 1949–1960.—v. 2. 1960–1971.
    1. Welch, Lew—Correspondence. 2. Poets, American—
20th century—Correspondence. I. Allen, Donald Merriam, 1912–
II. Title
PS3573.E45Z48   1980   811'.5'4 [B]   79-21574
ISBN 0-912516-41-0 (v. 2)
ISBN 0-912516-42-9 (v. 2) pbk.

Contents

I REMAIN

VOLUME TWO

1960
(Continued)

FROM THE NOTEBOOK LOG OF A HIKE UP THE JARBIDGE RIVER GORGE IN NORTHEASTERN IDAHO, 1960 [?]

1st Day   20 chukkers in one flock
          Juniper camp
          Columbet Creek? Seemed too far

2nd Day   Island Camp
          one doe
          fish full of gravel—eat those gravel covered
          worms. Heavy scales for trout. Lost 18 incher.
          Learned these trout have tender mouths.
          Dorsey creek? By large grove?
          Very hard going. Finally walked *in* creek
          about 2½ miles.

3rd Day   Black sand by very deep pool. Large perfectly
          clear crystals cause glitter. Intend to pan
          there on return.
          Huge canyon. Caves
          Good trail from canyon after 2 or 3 fords.
          Base camp by huge butte about 1½ miles from
          canyon (upstream) & 1½ miles from Poison Cr.(?)
          20 chukkers. Momma & 10 babies also.

4th Day   Hike to Poison Cr.(?) certainly Art's(?)
          Canyon. (Creek cuts canyon entering left.)
          Fence by PC(?). Good trail all the way. Then
          canyon narrows again. Best fishing. 5 fish 12 to 14 inches.
          Small cave. Buzzard feathers. Deer droppings.
          Saw 5 bucks. Group of 3: 2 w/3 points, one
          big rack—maybe 6 points, like arms.
          other group: 2 bucks w/2 points a side.

Chukker = chukar, a partridge.

1

5th Day 5 weasels(?) at dawn.
     Bitter thots. Fished all day to dispel them.
     Found cave with boxes, tin cans, flour hanging
     in sack. Magazines on floor of cave. *Capper's*
     Farmer for May 1932. These guys are always
     throwing away boots.
     Used marvel fly—brwn hackle peacock: caught
     35 fish in 40 casts and the fly, which cost
     me a penny, would still float!

     Hawk-shped bird, brwn wings w/white bands.
     Insect-catcher, swift as a bat. Larger than
     a dove. Kite?
     water-skimmer

         (so shaped)

         ngt hawk
    then swoops whippoorwill
    high.

6th Day Crash of deer on river woke me.
     Climbed out of canyon after breakfast—easy.
     Many exits on left side
     Hiked back to big canyon to inspect caves.
     Huge. water-filled in spring. Berry bushes.
     Salmonberries, blueberries, blackberries
     everywhere—not ripe yet except the blue
     ones: maybe currants?

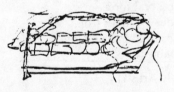

        house for miner.
        rotten canvas. pans
        & bottles.

    claim mark:

Am sure it's Dorsey Creek here.
Caught 15-inch fish w/marvel-fly. Even bigger

fish broke leader. Fly retired in fish-mouth.
He's rubbing his lips in the gravel, now.

Surprised Beaver who wedged himself under
a rock and drowned. Terrible. Couldn't get
him out. (didn't drown)
3-point buck
15 or more chukkers. A half-grown family.
Walked in clucking brood. Couldn't or
wouldn't, fly.

7th Day   Hiked to Poison Creek (about 4 or 5 miles).
Canyon gets very narrow after P.C. It's wild
and strange here.
Saw huge doe with 2 fawns

8th Day   Began hike out. Ford without changing shoes,
now. Much faster & safer.
Found Beaver o.k. he was asleep in his
rockhouse. Shouted, 6 feet from him, he didn't
even wake up.
Passed island camp tried for big fish, but failed.
Killed rattlesnake 3 ft long w/7 buttons

9th Day   Hiked to Murphy's. Took hot bath, swam.
Water too warm for real swimming.
Altogether from Murphy's to Poison Creek
should be about a 10 hour walk: 15 to 18
miles.
Roughest is from 2 miles past Columbet [Creek]
to 2 miles past Dorsey: 5 miles or so, nearly
all of it in the water.
Most beautiful after six miles—after Columbet.
Poison Creek and just before must be at least
a 2,500 ft. canyon w/many 3 or 4000 ft. buttes
in strange forms.

Whatever happens, happens so suddenly and is
over so quick that you'd have to have your
camera always ready—always sighted in. And
what if you could do this? Could walk all day
with a pack and cocked camera? All the picture
would show would be a very large doe and 2

fawns. The explosion in the brush would be
absent. All that noise as they break across
knee-deep water. The long hours of walking in
silent baked rock-cliffs of it—and you, tired,
with eyes stinging from sweat . . . It isn't a sudden
sight, a doe and 2 fawns. It's a long long
plotless movie. A man in a gorge.

To Charles Olson, from 1713 *Buchanan Street, San Francisco,*
9 *August* 1960

Dear Mr. Olson,   Just read your letter [of 6 May] to Dave Haselwood praising my poem and want to use this as a way to start
writing you—something I've wanted to do for some time. Thanks
for the appreciative remarks—coming from you, they mean a
great deal to me.

You "missed my previous stuff" mainly because all through the
dark early fifites I certainly didn't want to appear in any mag. I
knew of—went underground, tried to keep writing despite the
carping and all. I don't have the strength of temperament to go it
alone. What happened was a gradual retreat into overplainness
and severe constipation. Chicago. Where 10 lines a year was
pretty good production and people honestly used to challenge me
(as I tried to get on the way to talking about something) at the
level of whether or not there was such a thing as "pride" and
"truth." Poor babies, they honestly don't know.

Then began reopening correspondence with Whalen and Snyder (old classmates from Reed where we really had something
going about 1950—comparable, but smaller and different, to the
scene you got under way at Black Mountain—our Buddhas: Stein
and Williams: trying to learn to trust our own ears and breath).

But I strayed off into the bleakest regions of 'Murca and let
them badly bend me around for awhile. Then huge rebirth in
1957 or thereabouts: 80 pages of damned up stuff squirting out of
me in about 30 days. Whalen, it was mainly, that got me valves
unglued again. Then back to these mountains, this coast which
made me. It's been real good lately.

Enough of this—as the mad old Kraut says "stop yammerin'
about how you got out from under it all. All I care about is your
masterthought."

4

Am now working along the path started in *Wobbly Rock*: trying to set down the truths I learned from Mahayana—but religiously straight (no reliance upon Japanese forms, images, things). It must be made in terms strictly found in my part of this planet—to use yr. phrase, the "breathing" must be ours. The gesture ours. Our rocks. For this is how I know it and "after all you can only tell what you know in the only way you know of telling it. Of course, it may not interest anybody, in which case too bad." Only I know (just as she did) that it's almost sure to interest everybody if done truly. So I have always gone only on the standard of accuracy. If it is accurate there will always be form. If it is accurate there will always be beauty. If it is accurate it will have to count. So it's fierce and starkly simple: you don't have to worry (or even consider) these things.

Which is why I especially prize yr. remark: ". . . such individual acts (instead of the whole damned heavy machinery of the age etc.)." I come on pretty quiet for lots of folks right now. And while I'm definitely the sort that feeds on, that gets big nourishment from the wilder temperaments that got us off our asses, still I just ain't of that breed of cats (though too nutty to get jobs and/or impress our $20,000-a-year-cold-ladies). It's a very exciting time. The whole thing rests squarely on self/other. The bone is perception. The strongest stance of mind: the alert repose described by all them swingin' Asiatics who not only made it, but who so lucidly tell us how they got there. Anyone can SAY "there is no separation"—the point is to PERCEIVE this, knowing you perceive it, and not (somehow) letting this knowing fuck everything up. Fascinating exercise! Crazy university of endless courses and no diploma! All process (the rub—only the rubbing!).

And yet, as I've been insisting to Duncan in a recently started correspondence, the poems must be *about* something. Naturally. It's the *weddings* we record. Now we might (as we all do) spend fascinating hours with Gertie's *essence of the going*—but man, that gas is always the same. What I want to know is WHAT'S GOING ON OUT THERE? Like those satyrs you saw on that beach. Yes!

(always remembering there is no separation)

Right now it's a book on self/other: LEO POEMS: THE BOOK OF LEO WITH COMMENTARIES BY A RED MONK

I have a quiet room and this magic typewriter (a new Royal: notice the type face? The pretty "k" etc?). I have no excuses.   Lew

"those satyrs": "The Lordly and Isolate Satyrs."

5

Dear Gary,   You're right, "must quit waving arms and legs around."
Back in S.F. now, in my old room with the burlap. Have this new
typewriter, notice the new type face. No excuses. S.F. seems, as
always, to be peopled by vast numbers of folks who stand around
with expectant faces and droopy arms, waiting for someone to
rush in and "do" something. Eager to join anything *moving*. It's
easy to let this inert mass bog you down — easy to become flattered
by leaners: "Hep me take my cats to the vet. Shall I go to the
doctor? Will you drive me to Subud?" One must learn to shut his
door.

Will prolly work 4 hours daily in Post Office. Other, more
romantic, possibilities seldom pay $2 an hour and, after all, aren't
really available — you have to worry and fuss to *make* them happen,
which they do rarely. Tuna fishing. Grants. Etc. Etc.

Did not get my Saxton grant, so see no possibility of getting to
Japan (unless, which is imminent, my great uncle dies *and*, which
he possibly won't do, he includes me in his will — haven't written
him for years and years. Nothing to say).

Thanks for generous remarks about *Wobbly Rock*. Pleased that
yr. pleased with dedication. Huge response to the poem: inordinate-
ly flattering letter from Olson: ". . .delicious things go on in it . . . as
nice a new thing as I have seen . . . very true & delicate. Very
great." (wow) Like being praised by Bird. And today D. Allen said
more people mentioned me as new find etc. in his anthology than
anybody etc. etc. It is all very pleasant but remote, somehow.
Somehow is talk about what they invent I stand for, for them. It
removes something I used to worry about, though, is *freeing*.

Albert is in the vet's hosp. with hepatitis. Maybe won't be out for
months and months. He has bad luck and they fuss with him so.
This comfortable house may close down — lease coming up and no
one wants to sign it. Maybe I will. Or, when Kragg gets back in
Sept., may try to get long lease on cabin (bypassing that ass down
the hill). If Marin-an gets thus going again, & if it's my say, no
zazen! Will fiercely discourage everyone. Will allow anyone to sit,
naturally. But no hours. Enforced gate-waiting, even, maybe. Damn
it the fucking bench warmers and menopause people are only
drags. It was a drag at the end. My fault, in all likelihood. I was
much too gentle and wishy-washy.

Am writing and writing. Everything fine. In mountains all July and most of June: Sierras and canyons in southern Idaho. Lean, brown, tough as a jack rabbit, off the lush.

Hello to J. Eliz. (the silent). Met Cid Corman. Fine fellow. Have a growing respect for Duncan. Wish you could have been with me in some of that zany, dry, baked-rock canyon country I was in. What is scree? Smaller talus? When will we ever meet again?

(that animal we saw in Spirit Lake was almost certainly an otter)   Lew

To Dorothy Brownfield, from 1713 *Buchanan Street, San Francisco,* 24 *August* 1960

Dear Mom,   Sorry I didn't see you when you came through here, but I'll almost certainly be in town when you return. Call me at Jordan 7-7073 and we'll go out to dinner etc.

I was in Big Sur. Kerouac came by and we spent several days seeing everybody—finally ending in Los Gatos to see Neal Cassady, the guy *On the Road* has for its main character, and then went on to Big Sur for a weekend at Ferlinghetti's cabin. At one time there were 6 major American poets on the beach together thinking "one great sea wave could almost destroy Licherchur." For the time being.

Things are working out quite well. Have my old room back at 1713, will get a Post Office job within a week or two (reactivated an old civil service exam I took and am waiting for the call). Will work 4 hours a day at $2.16 an hour and will have money and time enough to get my work done. Nancy Welch still loves me, other girls are around, I'm slowly getting over the embitteredness I was gradually feeling about women—a great relief.

This house is too noisy and depressing for permanent residence, but will do for now. Several possibilities are around—among them the Mill Valley cabin. As soon as I have a small salary coming in all that will work out.

Albert claims everything is fine at the hospital, but I get a bad intuitive feeling about it. Vet's hospitals are depressing and dead. A bad place for good sensitive persons. Still, he will no doubt endure.

I really enjoy this typewriter. At first it almost intimidated me:

I'd strike the "e" and giggle with joy, it was so pretty. But now we get along fine. It's the best typewriter in the whole world!

I hope you enjoy your stay in N.Y. Tell me about it. I didn't like that town my last visit, but I look at things at my different level—which has little to do with how much fun it can be to visitors.

I find myself surrounded by good friends, respect, love, fame, etc. etc. I need this. Will stay here for several months and get my work done—trying also to get a life-pattern going which I myself manage, and which makes sense.

S.F. is its usual beautiful and cool self. The demise of the Giants is incredible—how to lose with such brilliance so often!

I got the package. Wear the jacket. Will wash Willy. love, Lew

Jack Kerouac described the weekend at Bixby Canyon in *Big Sur*.

To Dorothy Brownfield, from 1713 *Buchanan Street,*
San Francisco, 9 *September* 1960

Dear Mom, Thanks very much for the $25—I know it must have been something of a hardship to you.

I still haven't had word from the Post Office, but we must be patient. It generally takes this long, or longer, so there's nothing to worry about. Meanwhile, I hang tough—living here at Buchanan, eating well, and living simply.

It looks like we may lose the Buchanan house. Nobody really wants to live here anymore. It's dark and gloomy and neglected. All it would take to keep it and get it back into livable shape would be 2 or 3 people with steady jobs and some interest—paint brushes and a little love.

But it will probably just dissolve.

Today I'm going out to Mill Valley, looking for some places there—perhaps to talk with Kragg about the Dharma cabin. Jean Greensfelder took the census out there and found several deserted places she wants to show us.

Jack left for home in Long Island. He was in pretty bad shape this time. Utterly exhausted both physically and mentally. I tried to talk him into going to a rest home—which he could easily afford—but after almost agreeing, on a bad day, he obviously thought it was shameful or wrong—lacked the real desire just to sit still and heal. I worry about him, but he's amazing—will probably come out of it fine.

Everything is fine with me. I've written 2 long poems and 2 short stories. I'll have to let the novel go for a while, I have no confidence or interest in it. Will try to sell some stories.

Am having a dandy love affair—the easiest, most undemanding thing I've ever known—very satisfying and good for me.

Thank Lady for her letter and tell her to write when she can.

love to you both,   Lew

To Will Petersen, from 728 Plumas Street, Reno,
22 September 1960

Dear Will,   I enclose a poem which is largely due to you, though the immediate intercarry was Gary, you being the "Berkeley painter I never met," who showed me Ryoanji in your beautiful article in *Evergreen*.

I am really sorry I didn't meet you and your wife during your brief stay in S.F.—I knew you were coming and meant to arrange contact, but everything is happening (delightfully) at once for me, and I understand how busy you were.

Cid [Corman] left today (from Reno, where he read well, well received, off to Salt Lake in his several shirts and sweatband rolled over his belt, pockets full of books he gives away, tiny glasses, excited, seeing and horrified by old 'Murca, the shiny . . .) and it was seeing him again that brought you to mind. Then (as these things so often are) I came across that article of yours while packing my books here where my mother lives—I, moving her to another house in Reno, the reason for my being here to watch Cid read.

It is becoming increasingly more impossible to live in this country, as you no doubt noticed on your trip, and I hope to (somehow) get to Japan and not come back.

If I do that, I will finally meet you. We will endlessly talk about everything. Meanwhile, thanks.   Lew Welch

Will Petersen's "Stone Garden" was published in *Evergreen Review* 4, 1957; Lew Welch refers to him in the second section of *Wobbly Rock*. This letter was not mailed.

9

Jim, Horrified to see the clock at the bridge: 6:00! Thought it
might, at the worst, be 4. Please feel free to kick me out earlier
next time—I don't want to ruin your days, as I must have, sorry.

Would it be too far out to put the *Diamond Sutra* in yr book?
The best example ever written of a work that drives the mind
away from its words and back into the wordless world. Never
goofs. Real scary.

Here's that poem of Whalen's I garbled:

HYMNUS AD PATREM SINENSIS

I praise those ancient Chinamen
Who left me a few words,
Usually a pointless joke or a silly question
A line of poetry drunkenly scrawled on the margin of a quick
                splashed picture—bug, leaf,
                caricature of Teacher
    on paper held together now by little more than ink
    & their own strength brushed momentarily over it

Their world & several others since
Gone to hell in a handbasket, they knew it—
Cheered as it whizzed by—
& conked out among the busted spring rain cherryblossom
    winejars
Happy to have saved us all.

If you want a big chunk of Stein, suggest "Composition as Ex-
planation" as perhaps the best choice of a thing of hers that does
both jobs well.

Sure enjoyed that evening. Sorry I was so high and inconsider-
ate. Will write from Oregon. love, Lew
[P.S.] Reed Re-Returning Reading—readings maybe Reed &
Seattle with Mike McClure.

Also (very important) read Chas. Olson: "Projective verse" essay
in back of Poetry Anthol. It's what we all work from, now, & may
be important to reprint in yr. book [*Reading for Rhetoric*, ed. by
Shrodes, Josephson and Wilson, 1960].
[Enc.]

"I am not the house I carry about with me,
And nobody is really at home."

I said,
And was still unable, out of fear for it,
To make a simple rock climb.

I can give you, therefore, no ecstasies. It
Was only a perfect morning:

> head in the shade
> body in the sun
> slow sea lapping at the sand I laid on

Thinking (I was in that part of the world for a Jazz Festival):

> "Nothing we invent (including Jazz)
> (including this I've made)
> (including all you make of it)
> "Has anything to do with this . . .

When over the cliff's edge appeared two young beautiful people:
A couple I'd met only the day before.

And we were so glad to see each other.
And it was such an incredible accident to meet that way.

But it was a quiet thing—having to do with the way the sea moved

And when the time came we left together
To hear our greatest musicians.
And were moved again, in that different way . . .

> not to be confused
> we must somehow learn
> not to be confused

Left a universe for a
World of words, for music is still in the world of words,
And it didn't happen as it so seldom does:

> so seldom the grace of a chance meeting in a chosen place

Art is the enemy. Invention the enemy.
As muscles to the leap.

(not necessarily UP you understand)

Lew

To Dorothy Brownfield, from 2273 *California Street,*
San Francisco, 10 *October* 1960

Dear Mom,   I waited this [long] to write because I wanted to be able to tell you how the stove-selling went. I finally sold it for $110 to a man in Berkeley who will really enjoy it I'm sure. I got the grease can, thanks. So after I paid off my debts I have about $55 left — enough to last at least a month.

It is the first time in my life I've ever had money with absolutely no binds on it — either real or emotional. For example I don't even have a room of my own, no obligations, no set pattern in which the spending would occur. All that. And the Fromm "Escape from Freedom" thing is not working very strongly. So what I think I'll do (after looking over all the endless, infinite, possibilities) is: I'm going to Portland with crazy Jerry Heiserman. While there I'll try to get a reading at Reed: re-returning Reed reading, and possibly at Seattle, too. It will be fun and beautiful. We plan to buy about $20 worth of camping food and toodle up the coast very slowly, fishing in all the rivers — the steelhead are now running. Maybe take 8 days to get to Portland. Hunting for agates. Surf fishing. All that.

So I really appreciate you giving me the stove.

We came back here and went to the jazz festival which was disappointing, though there were endless strange people and beautiful. Paul met a lovely girl with gold hair and green eyes, just like his, it looks incestuous, and then (to make a long story short) after several weeks of bliss she left to go back to Santa Barbara and marry a guy she should have married the week she met Paul (probably explaining why she so quickly made it with Paul: trying to get away). But Paul followed her down there, hitchhiking with only 16 cents in his pocket, and got her back before the marriage could happen. He continues his strange Candide life. Everything different every 2 weeks. The proper exercise for people less than 25 years old.

Everybody thinks you're a real swingin' mother — which is true. It was very beautiful of you, the way you passed out those silver dollars and so nicely knew what we were about—however strangely we come on. Especially since the scene at Paul's house got ugly and square and loveless.

I have a great generous girl who is a sexual genius. But I'm too busy for seriousness in that area.

Jim Wilson's commission for an essay in a textbook (I'm sure you know of this) has me very excited. I've written the essay, from the poet's point of view, no compromises, and it's exactly what he wants. With luck the thing could easily mean $200 or so every year the rest of my life. How are your textbook plans coming?

So I'm packing Willy tonight and intend to leave tomorrow morning.

Glad to hear that you and Lady are happy in the new home. Everything is now better for me than it has ever been in this life of mine. Will write from Oregon within 2 weeks. [. . .] love, Lew

To Donald Allen, from 1405 *Southwest* 13*th Avenue,*
Portland, Oregon, 23 *October* 1960

Dear Don, Well here I am in Portland again after 10 years—the first return I have made in my life: I didn't even revisit Palo Alto where I grew up. There never seems any reason to go back to anything—like family albums: one is told that is him. It always makes me nervous.

But this one I really wanted to return to, Reed having been so good in my life and the Portland weather, the roses and sharp seasons (it was here I for the first time really lived winter).

It is astonishingly autumn. Today I saw a tree with strange branches that curved down off the limbs like monkey tail trees—and each branch furred with tiny leaves turned a yellow too bright to believe. The hillsides are all patches of blazing color with heavy dark evergreens pushing through. It rains. But roses are still blooming, and the weather is warm.

Portland has more fine Victorian mansions than any city in the West—probably because the millionaires here were a gathering from Idaho, Oregon, and southern Washington: Portland then as now the only real sizable place in all that area. We were lucky enough to get the attic of one of the nicest ones in town—a huge area with strange angles to the ceiling (highest point 25 feet) and triangles of skylights wherever the roof peaks oddly. I have an absolutely windowless room lit naturally only by a triangle of glass about 8 inches to the side—and this is 14 feet above me. The walls are not finished, just bare studs and laths. The room is dominated by the top of a dumbwaiter: a huge wrought iron wheel and many ropes.

Below us about 6 or 8 student-types are making their first venture in cooperative living—we remain just this side of sullenly aloof.

Below are ceilings with floral wallpaper, sliding doors 15 feet high, elaborate Danish steel fireplaces, fancy woodwork, and even a hothouse on the ground floor lined with steam pipes and floored with tile for growing orchids and tropical vines in rainy Oregon. Wisteria vines grow through the shutters so you can't close them. And all of it immaculate and clean and perfect—not the dim lines of what was, showing through neglect and years of boardinghouse use.

But Portland is only interested in its freeways. It is actually true. There is nothing, nothing, happening here except the building of more and more freeways. This house gets torn down in 1 year. A whole valley of such houses goes with it. All the downtown beauties are torn down (two I used to live in are parking lots now: small asphalt areas big enough to hold but 20 cars where once 3 stories of gracious buildings stood).

Most of my friends are depressed or bored—they wonder why I left what is their Mecca. But I'm enjoying it here, though I now have a bad cold.

There's no work except lifetime shots of one tedious kind or another and I'm down to $6—hanging tough, getting dinner engagements, trying not to worry. Am trying to get a reading at Reed for $25, and can read at a jazz joint for about $50. But these arrangements are going very slowly indeed. However, if they come through I will have another month. Food is very cheap here—a huge and marvelous farmers' market with horse meat for humans, great cheeses and vegetables, even real honest to god raw milk!

Am working on my stories now, after spending the past 3 days sweeping and mopping away at 100 years of dust—this attic has never been lived in. We found a box of rosebuds all tied in neat bundles—perhaps the secret treasure of some child, hidden and forgotten 50 years ago.

I hope I can persuade *Playboy* to take the voyeurish one I'm working on now—I understand they pay a grand. I won't bend stories for the titty mags, but if they turn out in their (I suppose) neighborhood, I will send them out their way.

My big plan is to finish this book of short stories and be able to say: "Some of these stories have appeared in *Evergreen Review*, *Playboy*, and *Field & Stream*." This ranginess would please me. And I have the perhaps naive hope that truly written hiking and fishing stories will go into the outdoor mags I've read for years. Gertrude's big ambition (realized in 1934) was to publish a straight shot in [*Saturday Evening*] *Post*. Remember it? It was all about money and ran several issues. The conclusion was "Money never changes, only the pockets change."

Which makes me wonder: do you think perhaps next time *Evergreen* could be persuaded to pay more than $5 a page? It would be so nice to sell something that made a financial difference. I am really responsible enough now to make $300, say, last for 3 months and produce huge torrents of goodies. Or am I being previous again? Or whiny?

The trouble is I know how many livings (such as ink manufacturers, etc.) are being made out of all this, and can't help wondering what the mysteries are. Have you found out?

Back to work now. Hope this finds you well. What gossip? What news? Lew
[P.S.] *Jerry sends love*

The "voyeurish" story: "The Late Urban Love of Peter Held."

To Gary Snyder, from 1405 *Southwest* 13*th Avenue, Portland,* 5 *November* 1960

Dear Gary,   Have been going all directions, so couldn't write sooner. Now am back in Portland, my first return to a past (usually can't see any reason for it, being someone else already) & find the experience delightful. Had a reading at Reed. Yr. poems, Phil's & mine, to a small audience at 25¢ & sold 8 or 9 *Wobbly R's* so came out w/21$. Thot I might be able to live off pen here, but it is very tough. Sold a short story to *Evergreen*, watch for it.

Reed still seems to be lively despite all alums opinion to the contrary. Different, sure, but what ain't. Not worse at all. Angels all over the place. I may be in love again: she's 18 and I hardly know her yet, but yew know how I do go on.

Lloyd [Reynolds] still roaring away, all the great kids love him—all the faculty wonder why. New guy on staff, Ken Hanson, a fine poet: read him in *Northwest Review*. Durham is running a jazz joint, The Way Out, where the best big band in America is playing. They aren't making munny. Hoodlatch has baby girl, is working all the time. C&B Baker have 2 babies, boy real nice guy, we go bb gun hunting together for bottles & cans.

Phil went East for a paid reading tour. Am trying to set up something here for me and maybe Mike—can read in Seattle for no munny but refuse to work free. Can't get free gas at gas stations, why work my pumps free? Beginning to realize that bad poet-pay is partly our own fault. *Evergreen* almost insulting, really: $5 a page!, bet the ink costs more.

Trying to get huge book of short stories off me mind. Secret plan is to sell at least one story to: *Evergreen*, *Field & Stream*, *Playboy*, & *Fantasy & Science Fiction*. Think this ranginess would be fun & wd. help put across integrated book. Also want to see if these mags can be persuaded to accept straightly written shots in their area. Think they might. Novel seems dull and bad right now, so am using some stories from it, junking (for now) the rest. Poems leak out fairly steadily, but I sound like a philosopher. OK I'm a philosopher, who am I to tell the poems how to talk? Will have to invent whole new form and also solve every Western problem concerning IN&OUT, Self/Other, Spectator/Spectacle, NoMind, etc. etc. somehow avoiding all semantic traps (HELP!) but can't avoid it, I've always been an explainer.

Very happy. I am now a happy man. No hang-ups, bad cough, poor. Worry sometimes about munny, worry hard in fact, but then wait, swing, somehow it goes on whether I pay for it or not. Tonite found 50 lbs. of apples on a tree in the zoo. Drink buttermilk at the B. Corner. Friends feed me. I fart constantly—praps me liver still? Am again sexually successful, girls desire me, I like that. I used to talk too much. Now I fart too much.

The Tao provides: found the best place to live in all of P., acres of room in beautiful Victorian house: Ladd mansion on 13th & Columbia. $7½ a mo. apiece for J. Heiserman and me. Have our own woodstove, free wood, unfinished walls, few windows. You walk through elaborate Victorian scene full of youths making a sorta co-op scene, open a door onto a mountain cabin at the top floor, replete with J's Nazi flag (burned & still 8 feet long), cheery woodstove, strange junkyard items J. finds amusing—my room

16

spare & lovely. I read, write, we go out and play, Jerry makes constructs of junk, paints, plays drums, dresses funny. S&F signifying Nothing, the sound of the true state of all living things: steady, purposeless, din of joy (last from end of funny story I'm now writing: "Shamansville").

Everybody wonders whether you'll ever come back. "For what in this country, except maybe the country?" I ask. Look for a letter from fine guy: Chuck Majisto (or sumthin'), who read D[harma] Bums, had dad read it, then they climbed Matterhorn. Wanted to know what face you took. Told him to ask yew. Gave address. Your myth all over these mountains, no need to come back—& it *must* be better there. The *instant* I get bread, off I'll go to Japan too.

It's really getting all glued shut over here. Very interesting. Meanwhile, large group of truly liberated souls wander about smiling and being outrageous. It will all fall down, say, in 5 to 15 years—or weld itself into a buzzing lump of no interest to anyone. Everybody wonders where Jackie and Pat buy their clothes. After debating on TV our leaders hug each other, smearing makeup on theyseffs. All issues are forbidden in the debate, because it's all too crucial to allow for party differences. It is so crucial, we are told, that it has all been decided beforehand, but vote! I understand people over there assassinate people. How barbaric.

Portland is sacrificing All for Freeways. No other activity. All the mansions must come down. This one goes in 3 years. Meanwhile the shamans are noisy amid the riches of what was once the greatest nation in the world. The riches turn out to be old—crafts having been lost some time ago—so that only the very poor, or eccentric, can surround themselves with shapes of elegance (soon to be demolished) in which they are forced by poverty to move with leisurely grace. We remain alert so as not to get run down, but it turns out you only have to hop a few feet to one side and the whole huge machinery roars by, not seeing you at all.   love to you both   Lew

Snyder used part of the last paragraph as epigraph for "Night Highway Ninety-Nine."

To Jack Kerouac, from 1405 *Southwest* 13*th Avenue, Portland,*
5 *November* 1960

Dear Jack,   Haven't answered yr. letter till now because of huge
doings in all directions at most speeds. Am now in Portland,
Oregon, for some reason or other—enjoying myself immensely.

At Reed College read my own poems, Gary's, and Phil's to a
small audience which included at least 14 true angels. One is the
daughter of George McNeil the N.Y. painter who you maybe
know from the Cedar Bar crowd—understand he's having a show
right now at Weiss (?) gallery or somewhere. She's beautiful and
open and bright—a joy to see how people turn out from hip fami-
lies. Also met a guy named Chuck Majesto (or something very
close to that) who read *Dharma Bums*, then showed the book to
his father, and then he and his father went and clumb that
mountain just like you said. Gary is their very big hero. I told
Chuck to write Gary (he wanted to know which face Gary climbed
and how). And so on.

I live in a Victorian attic in town. Huge place all primitive,
which is reached by going thru an elaborate downstairs: all
fancy woodwork and brass gas jets still in place, and iron fireplaces,
and 100 year old hinges and shutters—then you open our door on
the top floor and enter a backwoods cabin: unfinished walls and
little iron woodstove and no windows and firewood stacked up
and packs in the corner.

There is a beautiful garden around this place with rose arbors
and tall trees, always dripping wet. But it's not real cold yet.

Some of the best jazz in the U.S. being played here in a few
joints. The rest of the town very square—spending all their
money and energy building freeways and tearing down America's
most beautiful mansions.

Am here with Jerry Heiserman, who goes around to junkyards
and finds ruined old rusted typewriters, exploded mortar shells,
Nazi flags, old photos of humor and horror, doorknobs, funny old
hymnals, and the like—and who then stacks all these *trésors*
around in strange patterns until his room looks the inside of his
own head and history. My room spare and monklike with a cube-
shaped milkglass globe for light and a candle in a blown-out
mortar shell which burst into a perfect rusted blossom.

Willy enjoys getting rained on every day. He sends his love. He
has new tires on rear wheels.

18

I knew you were having some sort of a breakup when we last saw each other, but what can anybody, even your dearest friends do except be there and not add to the mess—the trip something we all take now and then, maybe because we string ourselves out too fine. What Larry said about the dry wine is very very right—and when the old body starts screaming for help like yours was: not letting you sleep and bringing on the scares and deep depressions (for there isn't any difference between mind/body) . . . then the only thing to do is slow down, feed yourself, get back in shape. Or, to put it another way and to stop sounding like a nurse, you don't have the right to kill yourself, Jack—too many of us love you and need you around.

Evergreen bought that story I gave you: "Man Who Played Himself." Am writing short stories now and have the goal of getting at least one published in: *Field & Stream*, *Playboy* or some other titty mag, and maybe *Fantasy & Science Fiction*, plus *Evergreen*. It would be nutty to have a range like that & then try to sell a book to someone (since all the stories fit together in a big plan). Have decided my novel is badly written and (therefore) dull, so have abandoned it—will use some of its parts as stories in the story book.

Also am writing poems, but they're strange and philosophical and maybe will turn out to be a little wiggy philosophy book. I can't really help how they want to talk—just try to let them go & the form is strange.

Oregon is full of farms as big as 50 acres with houses and barns and chicken sheds and creeks and woods, for less than $10,000! If I ever get a big chunk of dough I'll buy one. What a state! Cheapest living in the U.S. They even have raw milk here & horsemeat for humans: yesterday cooked a filly fillet on the woodstove (Eudora) and it cost 28¢. Yum Yum!

Love to yr. Momma. Jerry sends love. Did you get to see Phil on his trip East? What news? What raw gossip?   Lew Welch

[P.S.] (thot I was signing a poem, hence the last name—cold & wild up here @ Portland)

To Donald Allen, From 620 *Cleveland Avenue, Reno,*
16 *December* 1960

Dear Don, Here's the story about old Peter Held. It may be overworked, but maybe not—right now I'm very tired of the damned thing—10 years in gestation & just won't go naturally right.

If you'd like to play *Paris Review*: the story was given me full blown one instant in 1950 while staring out the window of an apartment much like Peter Held's. Only I saw no naked lady. I saw the whole story & I wrote it, complete, 8 times over the years—all of them are failures of the worst sort. Also, I'd try to pick out single paragraphs of it while at work in Chicago. Some of those paragraphs were all right. But what has been difficult is to get the thing to hang just exactly where it wants to hang somewhere on the spectrum between fantasy and reality. It's further toward fantasy then I usually work.

Also what's going on is I'm finally learning how to write. That novel last spring really has only that value, a personal one, it got a lot of shit out of my head and it gave me a lot of practice at seeing how you can come at things, or out up from things, into words. And I'm sure I'm right in going after these shorter pieces right now—rather than trying to blow a huge monster full of everything. I should have written that novel when I was 23. Now I don't care about the autobiographical shot enough to keep pounding it into shape. The stance of the Jimmy Vahey story is what I like, now—where am "I" in that story?

I have a real need right now to blow "pretty." Remember that last paragraph from "Margaret" I was trying to recall? It goes:

> Sometimes when Margaret was alone in her rooms, drinking her single brandy before dinner or tailoring the dress she just bought, her mind would drift on back through all of life and time, to a vision of swarming cells in a hot and ancient sea. Then before her inner eye would pass the long procession of forms: crawling and sliding, climbing up the trees, coming back down to live upon the ground again, staring dully at a piece of stick and a broken stone. Until attention fixed at last upon her thighs, her fingernails, the intricate sewing and the complicated liqueur—the walls of her apartment where she lived her clean strong life. Alone.

That story, too, came all at once—while sitting in a fancy resort in northern Wisconsin and looking at the young starched hostess. It will be even harder to get down, because for one thing it covers 30 years of her life. I'm trying to make it as simple as Flaubert's *Simple Heart*. It has to move that way—through tiny precise paragraphs covering about 3 years every page. But it must seem to move slowly. If I move into the above ending correctly the thing will give the same vision of cosmic waste that I saw that evening. And it includes a very terrifying bit about an army psychiatrist on Okinawa—a story told to me by that friend "Sievers" who is in "Chicago Poem." (that part about the cells is wrong)

· · · · · · · · · · · · · · · ·

I'm going to send "Peter Held" to *Playboy* on the outside chance for getting the rumored $1,000. Then maybe I'll try *Escapade* or *New Yorker*. I don't want to sell it for less than $400, though I realize maybe I'm feeling too big for my britches.

You can keep the attached copy if you want to, I have another. What do you think of it?

· · · · · · · · · · · · · · · ·

I really caved in just before I got here, the same old symptoms but caught early enough this time. I've got to face the fact that my liver just ain't good—and that sweet wine just poe-laxes me out. Weepy, crazy, scared, sick-tired I get. But good food here and lots of sleep.

I feel real good now. Have a tape recorder at Mom's university nursery school. Also lots of paper, paints, room, privacy in same place for making batch of pictures for Ebbe's show. Will use tape recorder for "DinMovie" tape. Bob (Bill?) Branaman supposed to show up here for divorce-living, but not here yet—movie will be with him, maybe I told you. If not, will.

Had a very strange take last night. Big SANE feeling. Review of all files. Review of recent whaling about. Amused. Realized I haven't had a place of my own since July 4, 1958 (when I left my wife . . . and of course, not alone while intolerably with her, so put it back to 1955). How nice it must be to have a bathroom always empty. Serious SANE plan to arrange same somehow. Realized also I have no control of mental states, no ability to remain in any one very long, no desire for such control. Am almost certainly mad, kookoo, most of the time. Have marvelous friends.

21

I envy no man, living or dead. "All things arranged to complete and delight me."

This, or like this, after getting up at 3, puking, not being able to sleep till nearly 6, watching exquisite white cat racing about house breaking things, leaping, taking toke on catnip, pretending to hunt tables, my shoes, redwood screen.

Also take that Jerry Heiserman genuinely fey with strange power to force others into important lunacy. One becomes his host. A shaman. Benign witch-man. Totally mental. One realizes what a powerhouse Rimbaud must have been, with the thing working physically as well. Poor Verlaine!

If I can ever afford to live as I wish I intend to have [a] studio where Jerry can be trapped into using best materials, paints, canvas, inks, paper and all. Seeing it as similar to Ryokwan problem. He can't settle, but needs to blow more than he's now able. Will show you exquisite small ink-color piece of his with piece of pasted money in it.

Will return to S.F. about January 15th with car full of paintings, maybe a start-tape for movie, full belly, full beard, steady hands (now they shake).

Wishing you the Merriest of Christmases

&

A Prosperious New Year

I remain etc. etc.   Lew

The "Jimmy Vahey story": "The Man Who Played Himself." The story of Margaret survived as "Our Lady of Refused Love." Ebbe Borregaard was organizing a show of local artists at what had been Hyphen-House on Buchanan Street. "Ryokwan": perhaps Welch was thinking of the stone garden at Ryoanji.

To Jack Kerouac, from 620 *Cleveland Avenue, Reno,*
18 *December* 1960

Ti Jean,   Got back to S.F. from Portland and found yr. beautiful letter at my old address & that great opening about pissing in the bus & having a whole great bus all to yourself, also huge seasound saga surge of lost hairfoam weed . . . weed . . . weed . . . (to break into chorus).

Yes, that's the same Lenore [Kandel] in *Beatitude*, I showed her the letter and she was pleased. (to rhyme with weed)

But I can't ever tell you in writing (now almost done in, tired, brandyfull) about how wild in Portland it was. Giant Reed re-returning reading poems and fucking 20 year old girls and getting (no shit) asked twice by liquor stores if I was old enough to drink— me, beardless and 34 and white hair all over the head and booze enough passed through me to float yr. boat to *Inja* (slack-lip British reading of last word). Put it far too briefly that Jerry Heiserman and me put on huge circus. Fact. A circus. All you need for a circus is naked girls and clowns and lion makeup. 380 people came to watch it, we marched in huge parade with gongs and cymbals and a dead loon hanging upside down over the stage (just below a huge Nazi flag with burned edges). But there warn't any room to put on the show so we just milled around a while (all them folks gapin' at the nekkid girls, literally, naked) and then we walked out—tattooed man and all. The crowd, I'm told, stayed till 3 or 4 and had a ball——never really figured out what DaDa outrage it really was. They still and never won't know.

So say I went to Oregon, me and Jerry both bought new shoes, we put on a circus, and came home.

Well then I spent several days in bed with sexual genius Lenore, started drinking that Thunderbird I love so well, saw everybody in S.F. and then old liver just sank and crashed—I got all spooked and jittery and couldn't sleep. Lenore ran off with a (literally) Prince from Liberia or Library, the Librarian Prince in all gold trappings, away she went while pore ol' Leo sulked and sick didn't care really, too shot. But she came back and I limped home to rest and eat. Didn't eat right in Portland. You have to eat!

Right now am painting paintings for Poet Painting Show at 1713 Buchanan (now a beautiful spanking white gallery, all floors, run by Ebbe Borregaard, a fine and beautiful fellow—you wouldn't recognize that place once so gloomy).

Finished another story. "The Late Urban Love of Peter Held." Terribly pure. Am trying for *Playboy*, they say you get a grand, $1,000! Watch for that story I gave you in next *Evergreen*. Larry & I didn't see each other after you left—thanks for giving it to him.

New story may be sexy enough for *Playboy*, I don't know. It, and the one I showed you, fits into giant book of connected short stories which I'm dedicating to you. I see it as maybe 20 short stories with little inserts in between, like Hemingway's *In Our Time*. Can't write that Leo book. Like you say about you, I'M tired of myself. Am in the middle of third story, have most of the stories half-assed in my head, most of the inserts between stories written (small, one paragraph, short stories).

Also am working on huge screech of sound track for insane movie: "DinMovie."

. . . .

Could never tell you everything, so won't try till I see you next time.

. . . .

Well, in 1950 I thought: "1960, that's the year!" And sure enough it was. Don't know whether it really was, or whether maybe I just made it be, to prove theory. Anyway it sure was.

I will never complain again. Whitman put it right: "All things are arranged to complete and delight me."

Merry Christmas to you and your mother.

Do you realize that 1961 is the same forward & upside down & backward? What might we ever expect!

I'm healing here, eating and sleeping and painting and so forth, will return to S.F. Jan. 15th for fresh whop at it. Who knows?   Lew

To Philip Whalen, from 620 *Cleveland Avenue, Reno,*
18 *December* 1960

Dear Philip,   We again approach the solstice, the death of the God, the Birth of Something Else (because some things, like poinsettias, are coming on now as at no other time and our theories have to let that in—& because we know it will be all right again). And I think about old Tommy the St. Louian who pretended about getting by on "dried tubers" when really he was eating goose and cauliflower. So naturally it is necessary to send you greetings.

What can we say to them? (All evening I've talked too deeply to my weeping mother, me weeping also, trying trying to persuade her it is o.k. for her to find it meaningless, but not o.k. to kill herself on that, right, account.) It is so very far down, where the real talking begins—and it sounds like such baby talk both to them & to us. What to say?

And I found myself without being able to avoid it using some of yr. lines as a text "minimum bother to ourselves and everybody else" and so forth. What I said and what you wrote down got in there a little—at least at the last she was laughing, though terribly tired. We do this to each other. Ungluing ourselves helps. A little brandy and the Son who hated her once and who no longer does, and the Mother who gave him up only to find him returning with clay all over his $1.50 boots, talking (as she puts it) in an "over-stimulating" way.

It can be said on this occasion, when something that really happened (a year, a cycle, a growing up and a withering away) is ending and another (we have every reason to believe) is already muttering away underneath there and everything—it can be said that you spoke more of it more truly than any of the rest of us. And it is very nice, considering that nobody asked you to.

I suppose I just used it as an excuse, but the vision I had about what 1960 would be proved to be correct for me. It is as the old man said "Everything is arranged to complete and delight me."

I tremble before the possibilities of a year which reads the same backwards and upside down. Lew

[P.S.] I return about Jan. 15 with Jeep full of paintings for Poet Painting Show. I needed this food & rest—exhausted when I got here. O.K. now. Best to Les [Thompson].

"dried tubers"—from *The Waste Land*; "the old man": Walt Whitman.

To Donald Allen, from 620 *Cleveland Avenue, Reno,*
29 *December* 1960

Dear Don,   Here's latest poem finally put in presentable shape.

Isn't this a fine new scroll-mailing technique? Tube is from paper towels. Mother uses at least 12 per year. Endless supply.

Do you want to send this to *Evergreen*? Or should I send directly myself? Please be frank, I am only thinking about possible wishes on your part, political or anything else—and admit my total ignorance in these matters, even to the extent of not knowing what yr. present connection with *ER* might be, or what you might wish to maintain or establish etc.

At yr. service. Will be in town about Jan. 15. Love. Happy New Year. Etc. Lew

[P.S.] To reinsert scroll into tube, twist scroll into tight shape using index finger in *inside* of loosely rolled scroll. Twist until scroll is *too small.* Insert scroll into tube and watch how it snaps into exact fit!

"latest poem": probably "Hiking Poem / High Sierra."

To Philip Whalen, from 620 Cleveland Avenue, Reno,
29 December 1960

Enjoyed your happy letter, Philip, one hears mostly exquisite worries in this house. And the ability of humans to invent these subtle means to their own destruction is becoming such a drag for me, that I fear I can't find much compassion any more. As you say, the EatWet house has a bland madness in it that is quite tiresome— there are so many happy ways to go kookoo, but it seems to frighten them unless they choose some unhappy one. As a late master of such luxurious techniques, I am perhaps oversensitive and under sympathetic.

But don't you think FOOGBOOK is going too far? (I find myself wincing as you did when I announced the title to my Reno story: *Shills like White Hierophants.*) Tenny rate I wait with the same hopes you speak of for the day when what you call your ice-block (if it's really there, which I doubt) melts away. (How's *that* for a sennence!)

I have a very vivid vision right now of what has always been the case with Makers of all sorts. EVERYTHING that has ever been said on the subject is not only wrong, but opposite, the reverse, an accurate statement for maximum befogging, an undeliberate attempt to mask, not guard, the mystery. I KNOW this to be the case: a few people get out of their own way enough to see how absurd & simple & joyful it all is. This vision cannot be revealed. It is possible to HAVE the revelation, but it is not possible to GIVE it out. It is, however, impossible not to SHOW it, in every act. SHOWING it makes everybody else nervous.

Tell Les that that is what is real history. Real history is endless chatter about SHOWERS (SHOW-ERS). A person walked about once SHOWING. Nobody will ever figure it out, but they are not able to stop talking about it. (Trivial example of real history: J. Eliz. Kyger walked about this city—everybody still talks about it. THEY HAVE NOTHING ELSE TO TALK ABOUT!) Think about anybody that ever SHOWED anything—that is what real history is.

Wittgenstein: What *can* be shown, *cannot* be said.

There.

Except that what makes everybody nervous is the solid knowledge that *they* can't SHOW it (it not being there). They keep playing Chopin pieces perfectly and then look up. They're nervous, the audience is nervous, because nothing happened and nobody knows why. On the other hand Chopin made them nervous because obviously something happened but nobody could say what.

Probably only the Buddhist myth-picture of many lives and final enlightenment and never the need to come back, but coming back anyway—all that—probably this is the only accurate statement of how real history *works* in any of us. We all grant that this is sloppy talking, but who cares how sloppy it is as long as it don't make matters WORSE.

Anyhow such is my desert vision (like).

Here's what I intend to do about it. I refuse the company of kookoo bores. Admitting my own extremely weak temperament, I will not let myself stay so long in turned-off rooms that I too get turned-off, sad, nervous, worried, bitchy, etc. etc. Should I become turned-off, sad, nervous, etc. etc. I promise not to complain—not to put *my* static into the already senseless din of the human world. I set aside all my former missionary-type drives. I will not try to *reveal*.

I intend to make my trip on this planet as pleasant and passionate as it is. I do not recommend my trip. Anyone is welcome to walk with me at times, so long as their own clumsiness and getting in their own way does not trap my very imperfect nature into its own tendency to mule and puke.

End of Epistemology Section. End of Vow Section.

· · · · · · · · · · · · · ·

Yr. report re: [Gilbert] Sorrentino's reading corresponds to Ebbe's recent complaint that his simple and beautiful gesture: the offering of rooms full of white walls to SHOW on—has met with Bitchiness from endless factions of artists. "I won't show if he does." "I won't show if he don't." Swish, gurgle, ffap!

The disrespect of our Community toward its artists is largely the fault of the artist. 800,000 people, 200 makers, 173 factions of makers. Mewl and Puke.

· · · · · · · · · · · · · ·

27

I used Ebbe's offer for a Poets' Painting Show to get me back at my brushes again. Have made many beauties. Painting is fun for me—I get so relaxed after wrestling with a tough one that there ain't nothing on my mind.

I may do more of it. As I've maybe said to you, I keep realizing how I don't really like words. ALL the trouble in the world is from words.

Now I hear that Ebbe has had to reschedule the show, in deference to bitch-artist-types. I'm truly sorry. I like Ebbe, and wanted his venture to succeed, but he is very dubious about it. Altogether he is a very straight fellow—one of the best of the young.

. . . .

Last night I almost finally got the "Hiking Poem" in presentable shape. Intend to go at it right now.

I sure wish I could have seen Mike's play. I'm certain it worked. They'll prolly talk about *that* real history for next 40 years. Good. It'll stop them from thinking about their little tiny hang-ups for praps 5 seconds running.

I've sort of sketched out "DinMovie." Now it has a conversation of a lady to her pets. Also a bit from a milk carton:

> By reducing the milk fat to meet market
> requirements, the percentage of protein,
> lactose, calcium, phosphorus, and other
> food elements is actually increased.

It also has people asking: "Do you love me, dear, do you really love me." And a real strange jewel. (Bark this out)
"Oh, so you're back! No wonder!"

•

Planning very exciting 80 mile walk for month of May in those strange deep canyons of Idaho. Have map. Am buying little things. Making lists.

Got beautiful weightless pack made for skiers—'cause I like to set up base camp and make 6 hr. overnight hikes out from it, carrying only lunch, fishing gear, first aid kit, etc. This pack folds to size of small sweater, fits easily in big pack. Delighted.

I don't think anyone else has taken walk I plan except one old indian. And he has horses.

Will show you map when I return (maybe Jan. 15)   Lew

Mike McClure's play: *!The Feast!*; "DinMovie" became "Din Poem."

To Kirby Doyle, from 620 Cleveland Avenue, Reno, 30 December 1960

My Dear Mr. Doyle,   What is a shame? Or, to be even plainer, *what* is "a shame"?

Referring, of course, to yr. curious missive with (thank you) enclosure from Wally [Berman].

Please relieve me of thesse horridd visiones (was it Mike's play that was a shame? Was Christmas again a shame? Are you all locked up? Did Dee go away? Did Officer Benbo finally *find* yew?).

Know that we live, here in the provinces, only on news from cities as great as yours. Realize that we need no wit—only the simple account of the events themselves will send us chattering about to each other's cottages. Agog.

Please.

. . . .

There are lots of calories here. The other day I won $50 playing dice. I sleep all the time. I stole paint from Mom's nursery school and have made some 5 or 15 paintings, all of them better than I used to make (in 1952 & back) when I worried too much. They are pretty. My mother is nuts, but nice. I got a new watch for Christmas. Hoping this finds you the same   Leonard

29

1961

To Gary Snyder and Joanne Kyger, from 2273 California Street, San Francisco, 3 March 1961

Dear Gary & J. Eliz, Here I am back in S.F. at the E-W House where everybody is out of work & the police keep closing in. We are all innocent of any even slight malpractice, but our irregularity of living pattern attracts much unwanted attention. Too much, too trivial, to go into here. /// Meanwhile the plums are blossoming in Mill Valley & I took D. Allen & Mike to Muir Beach, got lots of big mussels & had a nice dinner. /// Gary, we all want to marry the rocks at Muir Beach (perfect pair for it, huge) & would want to do the job traditionally. Can you send us description of ceremony, what ropes, etc?///J. Eliz., Don Allen is starting a magazine here in S.F. & would like to see large body of yr. poems cuzuv what Phil & I say about them. He is a *real* editor, so don't be too harsh on yrseff—send him enough so *he* can do that work for you (I say this trying to prevent, or minimize, hazzles, tizzies, etc. etc., trying to say: just bundle it up like it was in yr. wicker bag and send it). /// Gary, DA also wd. naturally want to see anything of yrs. Prose, essays, poems, takes, anything. Note: nearly all poets right now working in prose a lot. Fact. Are you? Corso novel, Doyle novel (nutty!), McClure sort of essays. Right now is time for yr. Tanker novel, which might go nice in mag. for prepublication publicity. I *know* you could make at least $10,000 on that & that you could, should, grind it out in one month. 'Murca now starved for good novel. Yr. skill, that story, yr. already fame, all add up right. Think about that. /// Don Allen is at 2370 Washington St., S.F. /// I am working on huge poem, stories-not-stories in novel? form (like). Am arriving at a bluntness that makes plain old *Wobbly Rock* seem flowery. Unavoidable. My way. I don't really approve of it, but will be obedient to the nature of the thing. Comes out that way. Also am painting. Not bad. /// Albert out of hospital, living with girl, fucking (by his own admission) too much. Me too! Perhaps I am in love. /// No work. No money. No way out. 'Murca badly depressed. Post Office so insulted me after calling me up for work (didn't like my hair cut, where I live, leery of frugality, thot me odd to *only* want prt. time job, demanding every address since 1/1/1937 for F.B.I.) that I could do nothing but refuse to work for the fascist sons-of-bitches. No jobs in town. Am trying to get by on yard work in Mill Valley. Everybody wants work done, but they're all too strapped to afford it. Am kind of a janitor at Batman Gallery (good gallery, good folks). Last month made $90 for story in *Evergreen* (out this month's issue, dig it). I limp along. Panic. Straighten out. Panic again. /// This envelope letter drives one into absurd compressions: game to see how much can cram in. Ignore present style. /// I wonder if I could perhaps fare better moneywise in Japan. I survive best on ½ bottle of hardstuff (gin Scotch etc.) per day, need at least 2 rooms (prefer more room), eat simply, like to entertain friends & travel thru the countryside. This runs close to $1,500 a year in States (if you live communally like I do now & am sick of). What wd. it cost in Japan? Could I get enough teaching work to swing it? Am serious. Wd. like to bring Lenore along, maybe. Might, sumhow, be able to raise boatfare. Have vision of myself in white robe w/rust sash & endless red beard, kicking stones on Jap beach, small-village house, red babies. Present status, though by far the best I've ever known, even enviable I suppose, is still not only not enough, impossible, humiliating, frustrating, wrong. This does not mean I'm even, really, depressed. Read it only as a hypersensitivity to the senselessness of human interference upon each-other's easy lives: the lead-pipe cinch made difficult. I just want to get out of their babbling way. /// The spring rains begin. In one month the mountains open. Plan 3 large trips, the last one in Idaho again. In May. 85 miles alone in them wild canyons I told you of. No one ever walked it before. Love to you both, [not signed]

The projected literary magazine became eventually the Writing Series.

To Dorothy Brownfield, from 2273 California Street,
San Francisco, 11 *June* 1961

Dear Mom,   Returned from sea to read your astounding news &
tried to phone Friday nite but couldn't reach you—so I guess
you're really in Mo.!

It certainly is a generous contract for the 10 weeks. And with
room & board paid for, you ought to be able to save enough to
help get relocated. You'll probably get very bored, but perhaps
you can get through it by pretending you're just doing research on
a strange race. This requires close listening to simple & decorous
talk about simple and decorous problems. All missionary work
must be stopped. In the provinces, attempts to convey a picture of
our partial enlightenment will only bring ritual death after mob
violence.

It is important that you take the above absolutely literally—
No Missionary Work!
(always, of course, being on the lookout for a glimmer of wonder &
intelligence from behind barbaric eyes)

This humble course of action can breed great compassion &
thereby mitigate the anguish of exile. An almost forgotten Roman
1800 years ago wrote from Gaul (in answer to a letter urging him to
return to silken girls & sherbet):

> They do not come to you at dawn
> Breathing out leeks and ardour—
> Great clumsy souls with appetites
> Much greater than your larder

I am writing this in the studios of KYA at 3:30 in the morning.
Lenore is making a tape as part of auditioning for a possible TV
program out of Los Angeles (a Schlitz-sponsored folk-song thing).
((My real pen ran out [of] ink so I switched to this one: another
case of inanimate object trouble which has plagued me all summer
with the boat & everything else. Now the mike won't work right.))

I haven't had a day off since you were here. I'm ragged & resent-
ful of having no time. Fishing is hard work from 4 A.M. until mid-
night with few breaks. Machinery won't work & sea lions steal your
fish. Salmon are always not biting or are biting somewhere else.
Fishhooks prick your fingers and knives slip, nicking your poor
swollen hands.

However, it is altogether beautiful & wild. You gradually reach a state of near nirvana:

> ". . . gladness as remote from
> ecstasy as it is from fear . . ."

Whales are always about, even as near to shore (10-15 miles) as we always are. Albatross zoom around. Sharks sniff at the dimple the line makes as it cuts through the water. The boat becomes an extension of your body—a super tool as close to you as muscles are—as eyes are. It is a strange encasement in an object suspended in the living void: just as being encased in our bag of skin is. You float, wheel, through a universe so real as to make the human world even more obviously absurd & petty.

We caught 1055 lbs of salmon at just under 60¢ a pound. It took six actual fishing days. The boat was cranky, but worked, on the whole, quite beautifully. One becomes very fond of the boat.

But the owner is upset at the vast amounts of money we spent fixing her. Tomorrow we meet with him & try to calm him down. Actually, all the work was essential. We did a winter's boatwork in about 3 weeks. He is such a fool that he may not be able to understand this, but we will try.

It is just possible that we'll lose the boat after all this, but that could be all right, too. I am now known to all the Nordski fishermen, & couldn't miss getting on one of their beautiful clean boats.

And the fishing thing could quite easily be a permanent answer to my problem of never having my life be my own. With a small boat I could easily make a good, free living—doing something worthy of a well-made man. Rare in America.

But now things are still uncertain.

I am very strong & well. Huge appetite (I eat about 6 times a day). Sunburned. Clear-eyed. Good strong rough hands, fingernails.

I enjoyed your split-letter. Lenore & I may very well take you up on your offer to play house in Reno. I am trying to find out if I'm divorced—if so, I'll marry Lenore, who makes everything work for me.

Then who knows? Maybe winter TV in Los Angeles, much money, spring Japan trip or back to fishing.

How I'd love to have my own boat, my own life.

So, all things considered, I still envy nobody who ever was or is or will be living. Whitman once said: "All things are arranged to complete and delight me."   Lew

33

To Gary Snyder and Joanne Kyger, from 2273 *California Street,*
San Francisco, 30 *June* 1961

Dear Gary and J. Eliz,   Again astounding news from Leosville, a
changed life, another crack at it from a different direction, a trans-
formation, a shed skin & exposed vitals: I am a Fisherman. Don
Crowe gave me the initiation by way of a boat he leased from a
fool who, after we totally rebuilt his boat & nearly (literally) died in
the process, uglily drove us from his boat & our livelihood. It is too
complex a story to relate here. We may sue for our labor, lost
income, assault & battery, & perhaps even slander. However, that
is mainly Don's undertaking since it was mostly his spent money
that is in question (+ his honour etc.). I emerge, as usual, with all
feathers intact & a bright eye—the shit washes off with one dip in
the fountain. Our trials earned us many friends among fishermen,
and one of them has hired me: the real invitation into a new world,
the acceptance, the reward. So here I am, boatpuller on the
Annie G. (Russ Moody, Capt.) waiting for the weather to break.
When it does, we fill the tanks, take on ice & bait, and head north
(or south, or, as we say, "out front": the Farallones, Pt. Reyes).
Annie G. is a double-ender, formally a schooner, keel laid 1925 (a
year my senior), powered by one of the oldest Diesels in service: a
fine old Atlas engine with comical rocker arms and long brass
external rods—like a giant museum-typewriter. Last trip the boatpuller sat in there twiddling a fuel valve with his finger in order to
get the boat safely around Pt. Reyes. /// I try not to become
unreally enthused about fishing, but cannot help feeling that this
could finally be an important way for me. The work is connected
with things I know are real: weather, animals, tides, fatigue, cranky
tools—the boat a giant tool, a connection with true history: centuries of courage & inventiveness recorded and handed down. The
work itself demands all that men can do, is a challenge to every
resource, requires being *with it* totally (not only the alert part, so
as not to put your head in the belts or to fall into the real void—
right there, just outside your new skin: the hull, the extension—but
also because you are hunting live things, so as to eat). There are
fishermen who "do everything right" and who still don't catch
many fish. There are fishermen for whom "boats won't work."
There are also great heroes, like Tony on the *Jimmie*: a man from
Nova Scotia who has mate's papers and who, the other day, fished
in a fog so thick it obscured the nose of his boat, alone, in a

troublesome sea, & who had a steamer come so close it cut one of his trolling lines, & who recovered this line (it had a float on it) & remained "on the fish" (stayed with the school he'd found) & caught 40 salmon (huge number) & found his way back to his anchorage by 3 in the afternoon: a feat comparable to "Mallory's Pipe" & far more complex, understandable to fishermen only. /// There is also the (pardon the expression) poetic part: sunsets, whales, funny colors, wild takes. For 20 seconds each evening the sea becomes a luminous gas of no-color: a thing to watch for & to usually miss in a blink. Drifting at night is the archetypical experience, too profound even to be mysterious. /// As I say, I try not to become unreal about this. Still, I dream only of boats (graceful, white black & red in Swedish style, perfect & clean). My wife in the foc'sle is cooking a stew which I smell just as the luminous moment occurs & a 50 lb. salmon (a "sundowner") strikes my line. All but this last fish are iced in my spotless hold & I in my Can't Bust 'Em Jiffy O.K. Beat Official Fisherman outfit clean my 50 pounder amid wheeling gulls as light fails, my muscles tired & my eyes clear & my heart full & calm. We will eat dinner and drift tonight. Tomorrow at dawn I will drop the lines, still "on the fish" who (as they do) will remain beneath the boat all night. This year we plan to winter in Mexico. There is a beautiful little village with adequate dock facilities. We lift the motorcycle onto the dock with my boom-hoist, so there's no transportation problem.   Lew

To Gary Snyder, from 2273 *California Street, San Francisco,* 24 *August* 1961

Dear Gary,   Things run all together & I lose track of time, so this letter may repeat some things in the last one. /// The *Annie G.* proved to be a filthy unhappy mismanaged boat run by a psychotic. It is very bad to ship out with a bad captain—perhaps you know. Anyway, it got very bad indeed and I got salmon poisoning on my left hand: a horrible mass of ulcers, like little moon craters, which, if not attended to, finally rot the bone. Now I'm cured of that & quit that boat & am fishing with Bill Yardas. Yardas is too much. I have, all this time, known for absolute certain that although what I thought fishing should be and what it actually had been were two very different things, that I was right, and the experience made wrong by nonswingers. With Yardas I am proved right. We wail around the ocean catching our share & more of the fish without 20 hour days, daily flips, disasters, frights, tizzies, & the like. His boat, the *Chico*, is clean and sweet to smell, fun to fish from, convenient & happy. We are right now catching the huge fat old salmon that are going to make the final river run very soon. Right now they "go up the river to take a drink": swim up a few miles & come back— milling around close to shore by river mouths. They are truly huge: 40 & 50 pounders at full strength. We have to shoot them in the head with .22 pistols. It is very exciting.

Lenore & I are saving half of everything we make—me fishing & she belly dancing at what was XII Adler—in order to buy a boat of our own, to be called *Capricorn* (after her sign: the Sea Goat & she very lucky and good with spells) although the final boat & the present bank account have the name *Lady Day*. But *Lady Day* will be a 40+ foot northern double-ender worth $10,000 & *Capricorn* will be a frugal & tiny little boat, probably from the Noyo River. In answer to yr. question: it is possible to actually make a fishable outfit for around $1,200. It will be 28' boat to 32' & will prolly be a little cranky & short of instruments. One would pull his anchor by hand & carry little or no ice (necessitating "day fishing": where you leave the city at 2 A.M. and fish till 3 P.M. and run back to city by 7 at nite, sell yr. fish & collapse—a long day—but it can be shortened as I'll tell you later, with more space & time at hand). Bill's boat is an ideal 2nd boat: costs $3500 to $5000 & carries ice and has more comfort and range and safety. Also, you catch more fish 'cause you have a better tool. Ideal boat need never cost more than $10,000 & is really fine beautiful solid & in every way a joy & a pride. Brass, oak, Australian iron wood, Monel, stainless rigging, Loran sets etc. etc. etc.: the Swedes earn & keep them— they are found in the north. /// My account is growing. I may be able to find first boat at Noyo by January with good luck and much perseverance & Lenore's help (I really don't believe I'll ever save enough, but am, now, anyway).

Thanks for kind remarks about Jimmy Vahey. My only right prose so far. I generally come on too heavy. Haven't read yr. pome about Hiway 99, but then haven't read anything lately. Worked 13 straight days, had yesterday and today off, return to Bodega Bay tomorrow for as long as weather holds. Did see yr. "Xrist," which is very very good indeed.

It is amazing how everything is falling together for me at long last: how it is the same as it always was, but now I fight it almost

36

not at all. In the midst of all the complaining humans do, I'd like to say I am glad I'm in this shape, here, on this little planet. It is a good place to be if you don't live *in* your or anybody's ideas. & wanting a fishboat & working for it is not living *in* an idea anymore than when that guy stared at the stick and a piece of sharp stone & started killing zebras faster for that hairy lady in the tree & that baby at her dugs. & I really doubt there are any but socially organized problems. It is a lead pipe cinch and people are miserable only because they are so overpowered, their brains and hands are so terribly quick & strong, that the simple task of moving around this gentle planet for 70 years is never seen neatly & in true focus & depth: it is too easy & therefore rejected. It is too much already there for the socialized brain to even suspect it. It all comes to this: I have no patience with myself miserable, or with anybody else miserable, if you get into this human shape, here, on this little planet, and can't make it, then fuck it. Don't whimper to me about it, I'm busy.

There is also something very wrong with being a professional artist. Anyway, it seems to me that even Whitman is out of focus because it isn't the same watching the wheat being harvested and actually getting the chaff in your collarband & Hemingway never hunted as an Eskimo does, for the work of it, the providing, & naturally never hunted with the same depth & skill.

I was really somewhat pleased that you quit the Zen Inst. It must have been an important drain putting up with that lady. And if you do get back here the fishing thing is a real possible way to get it all done in a few months, with all that winter for boatwork and diddling and writing & joy. The work itself absolutely necessary for all kinds of reasons. And it does figure out right in this bad system even: that with any real steady effort you *must* net $3,000 to $5,000 in 5 months even in a so so year. And the work as good or better than the months off.

Or say that it's wrong to be anything, professionally, as we say. A professional Roshi? A teacher? A fisherman? How can anyone so blunt himself?   Lew

"Jimmy Vahey": Welch's short story "The Man Who Played Himself."

37

To Larry Eigner, from 2273 *California Street, San Francisco,*
7 September 1961

Dear Larry, I've just gone through *On My Eyes* for the third or fourth time & want to tell you how beautifully I think you write.

For one thing, there is a speed in poems like the one starting "It's getting there" which I've only seen in Olson & Whalen, and I think you're even faster. By speed I think I mean only that really *all* the old lumber is finally gone, and that what is being got at is hit directly. The impression from that poem is exhilarating, a trip, a swift ride.

But it is a much deeper thing you do in the poems which, like your title says you are doing, speak in that big range just before what we see enters the world of words. I don't know of any poem in our language that does this better than the one about all that equipment about to work on that field, "the noise they make." (I just looked it up and find it's "the noise they were making.") & it's the look into that world which runs all through the book which makes it so astonishing and fresh and good.

But this is craft & the rest is harder to talk about: that I am moved by those poems, lifted out and shaken up a bit—something that after all is the only point to it. It is the big thing that you are doing (and I think what that is is the strong statement which translates out: "I walked about this planet for a while, it was this" or, like what Van Gogh did "I saw a sunflower, I Van Gogh," but I blabber, possibly).

I have to use your lines

> there are all types
> of an animate gaiety

as a dedication to a section of the poem I am now working on—a long poem about salmon fishing, commercially, the job I am now doing & which may finally have freed me altogether (or not). I will try to keep all my bitterness out of the poem—a thing you do so beautifully in yours . . .

As I write this my cat is nursing an old T-shirt of mine. He chews & purrs and kneads & today we discovered, upon lifting him up from these devotions, that he had his (perhaps) first erection. Now he has stopped. He sleeps in his flea-collar (September in San Francisco is the month of fleas: world famous). It is all about us, at every speed at once   Lew Welch

38

SECTION FOR FISHPOME

> *There are all types*
> *Of an animate gaiety*
>
> —Larry Eigner

Porpoises all the way out

I shoved fishhooks through herring carefully, the
Hook as near the tail, body straight (the bait can't spin), &
A pin through the head and hook
Tied with a rubber band

One after the other
Neatly arranged, belly up

Their bellies always white as
Porpoises, first, fast
White, driving through the water faster than you, then
Big black shape and splash

(Startled from herring, laugh, I
(Always feel lucky when they

Jellyfish, brown, like turkish pillows or
Ice-white in clumps of thousands, the
Goo all over the fishing wire, sting when
Splashed in the eye

"The slimy ones," filthy son of a bitches, nothing
To my knowledge, eats them

Green water, brown water, water with ⎫
Patches exactly like chicken shit even ⎬ PLANKTON
Feathers in it, the ⎭
"Penguins," to fisherfolk, murre, I'm told, up
To dry their tiny wings (stand like emblems on Roman standards)
& swim as fast as roadrunners run

        "caught one three stops down" (60 feet)

A bird on a fishhook!

        or the barnacles when we painted the
        boat bottom: cluster of them on the
        screw shaft. A whole life spinning! &

39

then I wire-brushed them into
void for how many Kalpas, the

Whole business very hard on sentient beings

It's all crowded around us as we walk our bellied floor

The salmon so big in August we
Shoot them in the head before gaffing them
Pounding their heads in, guts ripped out & thrown to the gulls

lice in the gills
lice by the fin behind their vents

Like tiny rays or skates

very end	"You can't do that and be a Buddhist." So much the worse for Buddhism.

next to end: No more fish to gut, the
                    Gulls ignore us into port

Or:

So
    much
        the
            worse
                for

Buddhism

· ·

at times a fishing boat is visited by canaries

· ·

"I had dozens of them once, albacoring, they
stayed with me 3 or four days, hopping all over the
place. One died in the scuppers. Just sat there
sleeping, so I didn't disturb him. Then, plop,
over he goes with his little feet straight up in the
air. It was awful. And not one canary has lit on
the boat since."

That's as far as I got on Sept. 6, 1961

40

[ON SALMON FISHING]

I

I'd like nothing better than to be able to start this like *Life on the Mississippi*: with a vision of the Northwestern salmon fleet sweeping toward the docks of a coastal town, gulls wheeling overhead, small boys running to see their heroes return with decks full of gutted and sea-washed salmon, docks springing to life, excitement in all the bars and young girls straightening dresses and making lipstick moues in front of upstairs mirrors—but I can't start that way because fishing isn't central or even very important out here. It ought to be, there are no true salmon in the whole world except those on the Pacific Northwestern Coast, and the whole world dotes on them—but it stands, the industry, as a remotely colorful collection of not understood boats glimpsed briefly by suited paper shufflers as they eat expensive dinners "down at the wharf."

I saw a tall man from Iowa who had never seen a sea-crab watch one being dropped alive into a vat of boiling water. He was both horrified and amused, backing away from the vat, laughing to his friend & refusing to eat so strange an animal. (I respect his country reticence.) And it is curiously common to hear some native Californian say, while watching salmon being unloaded: "What kind of fish are those?" or "Salmon? I thought they only caught *them* in Alaska."

*

Few people know that the finest fish in the world swim just off San Francisco Bay: the chinook, or king, salmon of the Farallones, north to the Russian River & south to Monterey.

Here the chinook achieves its greatest size and has its finest brilliant red color to its meat. The Farallones, a string of barren islands which are the peaks of an undersea mountain range 15 miles off the California coast, offer perfect feeding grounds for these magnificent fish.

The principal bait is shrimp—and it is the high iodine of this feed that gives such striking color to the salmon's meat. I have seen balls of shrimp rising from the depths like huge red bubbles, the ball a sphere of life 12 or more feet in diameter with dark shapes of feeding fish, mackerel, shark, salmon, darting through them and sending the tiny shrimp hopping about the surface like fleas. At these times it is possible to dip a net of cheesecloth into the ball and come up with 10 or more pounds of them, [each] only a half-

41

inch long and nearly transparent. We'd steam them in a few inches of sea water and eat them whole, heads shell and all, or, as one fisherman's wife did, make a delicious soup broth into which chunks of salmon or ling cod and potatoes were put.

You could seldom catch salmon when the shrimp balls were blooming all about the boat. Either the lines quickly filled with mackerel, and hake, or nothing happened at all in the midst of all that feeding frenzy. But it was more than enough just to watch the fury of the birds and fish and the strange rising little insects like swarms of underwater pink bees.

The really big salmon are caught late in the season, usually in July or August, and you seldom catch more than 6 or 10 of them in a day even with a commercial troller with 36 hooks trailing behind the boat. They are caught deep, 30 to 40 fathoms down and then on the bottom hooks almost always. Large wooden plugs, spoons or little rubber hula skirts behind foot-long silver "flashers" seem to be best for these fish, though large herring fished deep enough are sometimes good. You have a lot of trouble with lings and rock cod (delicious fish but worthless commercially unless caught in huge numbers in trawlers' nets), which strike the bait somedays almost before you can get the lines down. At these times, too, the water is often full of jellyfish which gum up the lines and bait and finally make fishing impossible.

Add to these problems the fact that the natural feed is tiny shrimp and, further, the fact that the salmon are beginning to feed less and less as they prepare for their foodless swim up the breeding rivers, and it is clear why these really monster fish are hard to come by.

The true Farallone salmon will run from 30 to 50 pounds or more, have huge humps on their back just behind the head, and mean-looking hooked lower jaws—like the oldest and biggest land-locked salmon. Strangely enough the very largest of them sometimes hardly put up any fight at all.

In 1962, after I had left the boat to try my fortunes in the mountains, Bill [Yardas] caught the biggest recorded salmon, taken either by sport fisherman or by the commercial fleet that year. Dressed, the fish weighed 54 pounds and might have gone nearly 70 pounds with his belly left in. It came to the boat like a puppy dog as Bill gently drew in the leader by hand (and it might be that it was his good technique that partly accounts for this docility, because rough handling will definitely spook your fish).

42

When he was finally alongside the boat, just an arm's length away and swimming leisurely beside the moving boat, Bill shot him in the head with the .22 pistol, slammed his gaff into his bony head and heaved. The fish was so heavy he could hardly get him into the boat with his one good arm and finally fell back into the cockpit with the huge fish flopping about on top of him, nowhere to move in the tiny cockpit.

It was a male. At the fishdock the Fish and Game People weighed and measured him and took scale samples to determine its age. "They're almost always males, the big ones, and usually 7 or even 9 years old," one of them said. "There's a theory that they're undersexed or timid or something and miss their first mating trip, get lost or something, so wait around another 3 or 4 years. You hear about them not fighting as hard as a 16 pounder." Bill used to wonder if maybe his fish was a queer.

It was taken on nearly the last trip Bill ever made as a full-time commercial fisherman. A good finish to his long years scratching out a poorer and poorer living in a dying industry, a dying sea.

*

I have lived all my life with people who will laugh at all of this, being too sophisticated to hear what I said except as "another plea to return to nature." But nature is larger than that, expressible in the word-game "Nature." It is all that goes on whether we look at it or not. All-that-goes-on-whether-we-look-at-it-or-not will always go on (though we almost never look at it) and we are in it, in this form, for a little while at least. There is nothing to join since we are as much a charter member as a jellyfish is, as the seasons are. The rest is what drives us mad. And you do know exactly what the rest is.

II

It is real work that I wish to speak of, and it's only natural to start by saying that hardly anybody knows it is still going on, that there are no salmon in the world except those on the Pacific Coast, the rest being various kinds of oceangoing trout like our Pacific steelhead, and that real work has a small place in America now, where there isn't really very much going on except the moving of baseball teams from city to city (mostly toward the West).

And I cannot keep this edge of bitterness out, though I resolve again and again not to let it in, because the bitterness is there: so many years working at foolish, exhausting, tiresome, humiliating jobs—the thing that has beaten this generation down to its finally clean edge. I am too much of a loner to try to say *we* about it, but it does seem to me that there are very few things left to understandably do, very few things that a proud and vigorous man wants to do. Every now and then I get the oppressive vision of what it is that a smart strong man might devote his entire life to Post Toasties or Prudential Life Insurance. Still, "a man has to eat," and we almost all of us spend our lives doing another's bidding, calling it "will" when actually it's only the fear of what we think another's will might be, driving us out of our beds at 7 in the morning to do the work America now does: 4 out of 5 of us not making anything, but only keeping track of things—shuffling the records about, or moving it from dock to freight car to warehouse to store, or selling it, or the idea of it, or managing it (whatever that might mean.).

It has to be shown against this desperate backdrop or what I have to say about salmon fishing, now that I'm in it, will only be another thing like "What's My Line?" or "People Are Funny." smugly quaint & ugly

It is real work that I wish to speak of: how it is to do a proud thing which earns you your house and your food and your woman; how it is to actually go fishing, that is to catch the fish for people to eat. . .

*

The boat I work on, the *Chico*, is a 32-foot salmon troller out of San Francisco. You can see it, most any day all winter and when the weather is bad in summer, tied up against the dock by Fisherman's Wharf—one of the hundreds of small boats that make up this part of the great fishing fleet of the Northwest. It's bigger than some, smaller than most: a Columbia River "Bar Jumper," not really typical of this part of the coast. Most San Francisco boats are Monterey Clippers—shallow-draft, graceful, old-fashioned little boats built on an ancient Italian design (most of the fishermen in this area are Sicilian).

Bill Yardas, the owner of the *Chico*, is a Slavonian, son of a Eureka logger. He grew up with small sailing boats in Eureka Bay, sailing all day long for no particular reason while I, for the same lack of anything better to do, played pool in Palo Alto. About three years ago I met Bill, learned he was a fisherman and envied him, and by a very improbable series of circumstances too complicated to go into, became experienced enough so that he could hire me. Now, as I say, I work on the *Chico*.

The *Chico* had its keel laid in 1918. Most of the fishing boats on the Pacific Coast are old, made of Port Orford cedar and ribbed with oak. There is no reason why a well-made wood boat should ever wear out if you keep proper care of it, and the *Chico* has apparently always had owners who care. This is one of the things I like about fishing, and don't like about America in general: when you are really fishing, that is actually catching fish for people to eat, you are dealing with material and machinery and methods that have nothing fake about them—they do their work and never, reasonably, wear out. Of course, there are right now a great many fake fishing boats made out of landing barges or Chris Crafts, but they really don't count because they are bad tools and nobody takes them seriously.

*

Life is all around us, going at every speed at once.

Last night we had to raise the anchor, move the boat, and anchor again, because it looked like a wind was coming up & the kelp we'd hooked in would never hold us. I stood on the bow, in the fog, watching for boats (many fishermen are careless about lighting their mast lights), sleepy, in my shore-type slippers. Bright streaks of it jittered out of our path as we eased along through phosphorus water. Their terrified little minds. What fish? (Must we always name them?) Then I let the anchor down into good sandy bottom and watched the rope go taut. We slept easily that night.

And the next morning I stand on our clean deck, made cleaner by the fog all night, and urinate over the rail. The burlap bags I put over the side to wash in the surge are still hanging from the rope I tied. I lift them out and find they're full of baby shrimp which hop in the meshes like little pink fleas. It's 4 o'clock. Dark. Bill is down below, fumbling with the diesel stove. I am bone weary after 13 consecutive days of this (you have to fish every decent day because the weather can always put you out of work & it's a short season). I always wonder if any other animal has to begin its hunt as painfully as we do. But the cabin warms up, the radio is turned on, and breakfast begins to fry.

The fishing radio is very strange. It's like sparrows waking up. In the San Francisco area the Italians are the first up—they fish in very small "day boats," selling their fish each day, not, as the "Nordski's," icing the fish for 5 to 8 days and selling them all at once. For this reason, the Italian fishermen have to get up at 2 or 3 in the morning and run out to the fishing grounds. The San Francisco Italian fishermen love to talk on the radio, particularly during those early, lonely hours. So you turn on the radio at 4 & it is alive with a babble as meaningless, and meaningful, as that from a palm tree full of sparrows at dawn. Through the din of Italian & good mornings & explaining how their lasagna was last night finally come reports of what the weather is like. Meanwhile we eat eggs. We are at Point Reyes, only two hours from the fishing grounds. They are running out from San Francisco. So the whole Northwestern fishing fleet depends on the Italians from San Francisco (that is, they depend on them for accurate weather news each morning when the fishing is near the Farallone Islands or Pt. Reyes).

These fragments were written 1961-1963.

1962

To Gary Snyder and Joanne Kyger, from 4120 *Geary Boulevard,*
San Francisco, 13 *February* 1962

Dear Gary & J. Eliz. Read letters of yours to others & got yr. address from Phil & found this air envelope & thot I'd write. Almost
immediately after writing you how everything was so great I (after
uttering such contemptuous things about people who can't enjoy
the human shape and setting) went altogether unglued ga-ga depressed and dead & flippier than ever even for me. No doubt some
hubris punishment or other. Better now, but keep disappointing
myself—I'll never learn, give up, make it, understand or anything
—but operate better this way, am nicer to others etc. til manic
frenzy again hits. Ah well. Bill & I went crab fishing, quit Xmas (no
crabs) but will start again next week on theory that even $10 a
week is better than starving. Then, April, saimon starts again.
D. Allen says he may be able to get an article into *Esquire* for me—
Salmon Fishing. A natural, but I can't get off my ass. Sloth. Sloth. I
sleep till 3 and play chess. Blah. I am the Buddha known as the
sleeper (in all senses I hope). Tried to go zazen every morning at
5:45 but am too slothful. Beautiful Bush St. Zendo. Soto. You
prolly know about it. D. Allen goes every day and is wiser and
kinder and doesn't have amoebic dysentery any more. A jolly
fellow. We go hiking to Marin all the time with half pint Jim
Beam. Bring back branches and shells. Lenore [Kandel] and I have
lovely suite of 3 rms. in a new East-West House (note address).
Lavender & white b. rm., woodstove, small rustic porch studio for
me writing. We rented out a studio to a guy who claimed to be a
painter & who got busted for showing dirty movies to 15 yr. old
girls—he and his wife "approaching" them the while. A great scan-
dal. I hope it's all a big fink lie—he's a nice fellow (as yo'all ken
see!). Saw *Origin* with yr. fine Hiway pome. Most flattered by dedication. Saw book J. Eliz. did for Jim Hatch—lovely. Found new
product: Nadinola, a bleaching cream for spade ladies—will send

J. Eliz. a bottle at once! Please look thru all history & find a saint who made it thru slothful behavior. But true slothfulness allows baths and *all* comforts, remember, am not interested in compulsive types. Maybe I'm just reacting from all that hard work last summer. Still want me own fish-boat. Also, while in big funk decided to give it all up and become teacher. Couldn't (thank Gawd) do it, however. Yours in sloth—Dudley Fieldstone

ACEDIA!

sin   sin   sin

"Hiway pome": "Night Highway Ninety-Nine." "Dudley Fieldstone": Welch's Reed College nickname.

To Dorothy Brownfield, from 4120 *Geary Boulevard, San Francisco,* 9 *March* 1962

Dear Mom,   Well, everything continues to be just fine, except the weather which is either wet or cold or both. I finally seem to be completely out of my blue funk, thank goodness, not that I really feel exuberant, but I don't feel all over crumby.

We didn't go re-crab fishing after all. It appears that it is not worthwhile. So, I tried to get a job at the Yellow Cab Co. & they refused, saying I didn't work every day in the world. Other offers fell through also & all that is left is a job on a yacht in Sausalito, 7 days a week for a rich prick who wonders (after a half hour interview) if I was "invited aboard."

And it is only 5 weeks away from salmon season, so I've decided to stay alive by borrowing money until then. I borrowed $50.00 from Phil, who got a nice $500 poetry grant, & have asked Albert for another $50.00. That will do it until April 1st, paying off my E-W House bill & buying food & paying rent & buying cigarettes. Also, I own 12 Bruce Conner drawings, a friend, and have put them out on consignment at Batman Gallery. If they sell at the price his stuff is going for (he's real *in* right now with the N.Y. crowd) I'll get $290.00—but that is uncertain. [. . .] *Write.   love,   Lew*

To Kirby Doyle [*from San Francisco, Spring,* 1962?]

Dear Kirby—Thank you for your accurate outrage at my real showing of lack of trust—however in sleeps it may have come from —it is there, in a little kernel growth on me lately & now (largely thru outbursts of love & its outrage as you showed, and as, lately, so many have showed) but now, it is *seen* by me & therefore destroyable.

It would be lots better if I could only flip some other way than this freezing of the outward go, but that is what happens, a re-coil, draw back and keep, fright of the mind and sensibilities . . .

So it was *keep car, keep car, keep* out of my tiny fright mind. No wonder it affrighted you . . .

And no allowable out that there I was in deepest sleep, out-mind —*For that is precisely my work!!*

and, Jim, if I can't work better than that . . .

My whole imagined world is once again destroyed by *KEEP.*

Keep kills me. Good.

Keep is the world my mother taught me to keep.

Keep killed Lenore's very big love for me.

Keep killed my love for her, that I wanted to keep it and

AM NOT A GOOD KEEPER!!

Keep falls off of me.

I will not keep me anymore.

NOR ASK FOR KEEP!

NOR GO *WITHOUT* KEEP

* * * * *

(line to be added to giant, all-inclusive letterhead)

ALL KEYS AVAILABLE

open

24 hours the day

(with luck)

Lew

L O V E

*To Dorothy Brownfield, from General Delivery, Big Sur,
California, 12 July 1962*

Dear Mom, Am now at Bixby Creek, borrowing the cabin of
Lawrence Ferlinghetti, poet & operator of City Lights Bookstore
in S.F. He will be here about July 22, at which time I'll leave here
and either come up to see you, or move in with a friend here in Big
Sur. In any case, I have enough groceries and cabins to survive till
August 1st or thereabouts. Write and tell me when you will move
& I'll help you & we can start on our trip etc.

There was no summons or warrant waiting for me, so I've
decided to ignore all that business. A gangster friend of mine who
understands these things better than I do, advises me not, ever, to
turn myself in. He sees it as a kind of ultimate *finking*. I am but one
of unfindable thousands, so why help them at their nefarious trade.

It is very nice here. I am beginning to grow calm.

Enclosed is the doctor bill.

Write me General Delivery, Big Sur, California. How are your
job plans etc.

Now I am going to take a bath at the hot springs. love, Lew

*To Dorothy Brownfield, from General Delivery, Big Sur,
18 July 1962*

Dear Mother, I just want to say how much I appreciate all the
help you've been to me. I've been in such a disturbed state lately I
haven't been able to say it properly when we're together.

My car, its marvelous 6-ply tires I so love and need, my nice new
moccosins (sp?, never wrote the word before), the beautiful
Pendleton shirt I dress up in . . . it seems that so many things have
come from you, and all of them lately. And this typewriter! How
could I get along without it? And every time I fill up the gas tank.

I do so deeply appreciate all this.

I was told recently by the one psychiatrist I talked to, that one of
my great problems seems to be the easy acceptance of love. It is
true. I often feel so guilty. It does me no good, and it certainly does
no good for the ones who love me and give to me.

As you said recently, I have almost cheated you sometimes by
not asking for help when I needed it. I'm sorry.

I've been looking forward to our camping trip eagerly. I have several ideas about your sleeping arrangements, for I do worry about having you cramped up in that small car. We'll talk about that. Also it might be possible to board the cat with some of my friends, though I can't promise this—so many of us live as unstably as I do.

And please don't worry about your job. Of course you will be always able to live comfortably—that's the primary purpose of your father's money. By all means, let's not cancel the camping trip on *that* account.

I have had a violent time of it spiritually, but it looks like I'm coming through. Breakdowns for others are breakthroughs for the Poet. It is one of our major jobs. It was absolutely essential that I have this time to myself, alone—it is the first time for more than 3 years (except for that short camping trip in Idaho). It is better this way—in a house, or, as this is, a hut.

Please write, telling me when you need my help in the moving. love, Lew

[DRAFT OF A LETTER TO ROBERT DUNCAN]
Bixby Canyon, July 1962

Dear Robert, It is odd that I should want to write this letter to you, since I know so many of us better, who I respect as much. But at this moment my spirit, what's left of it, needing to speak, can only speak to you.

I must speak to one who has gone through something as black as this, and who made it somehow—or at least is still there, operating his Human Being (your phrase) decently, as a poet.

I have reached what I hope is nearly the end of 5 months of a total withdrawal of all love, all spirit, all hope, all vision—my whole being drawn into a fist pounding bitterly against Everything, for it has seemed that Everything is dedicated only to mocking MAWKING all that I know is good, and here. I cannot shut out the din anymore. I am afraid.

The other night I miss-heard on television a fat trained fake-virile voice boom:
... OUTNUMBERED, AFRAID, AND UNCORRUPTIBLE
I don't know what was actually said, but now I use this as my letter-head (the couplet was not intended, I am not giving this letter, always, the care I give to my Writing—where I always hear the

51

music just before I find the words that sing it)

I will not list the details of my personal troubles, it's the usual list of details.

For it all goes down, now, right to the bottom. All action, all movement, sur-real scenes in an accurate movie—the cashier in the supermart, the dialogue in the bedroom, all true "literally and in all senses" . . . and it's important to remark that the "literal," the "stubborn fact" of it is vividly there for me, as I'm sure it will always be.

For though I am mad, I am mad in the way Poet is always, must be, mad. It is the difference (as Jung put it to Joyce, trying to convince him that his daughter was in grave danger, and Jimmie said "Nonsense, what you describe is what I do all the time. It is even a game we play together.") And Jung answered, "Yes, Jimmie, but you *dive* to the bottom of the river. She is *sinking*."

The poet can never sink and, while sunk, be Poet. His diving is always a dive, even if to do it he must sniff the vapors in his oracular cave—or otherwise drastically wrench himself open that the *whole river* flow through. (Which is what is wrong with Jung's phrase—he makes it sound a little prim: as if one could learn to mount the board, properly suited, spring a few times, and do the trick cleanly whenever one wills.)

And so I have not sunk. And the sickness I've been through had nothing to do with the bottom of any river. It was the worse thing: the deliberate *closing* of myself.

And I found that whatever it is that chooses to flow through me is so powerful it will destroy me if I resist it *in any way*. That I must open to it or die. And the death will be a suicide.

I opened to it 2 days ago, here, at Ferlinghetti's Big Sur cabin, after being alone for 5 days. It wasn't a clean opening. It was a pulse. A timid thing, like that way a trout lies still and timidly works his gills a while when you land one and then return him to the water.

And I got the most radiant vision of openness. I saw how this was all meaning. That I was only a mess of gates. That having Human Being is to have many many gates, that it *all* all flow through.

That it was all right, too, that we have a Self. That it *all* be transformed. Different on the way out.

And all of this was so powerful my penis came erect, with no sex to it, and, as the old saying goes "putting your prick through the window, and fucking the world" with helpless love!

What is this? Some black satori?

For I cannot stay open to it. It hurts too much. But what is it that hurts?

I have dropped all devices. I cannot even drink wine anymore. All last night my dreams were horrible nightmares: my mother and I and my best friend (who kept shifting, being all friends, and who I called my brother) left a movie and walked through a deserted, poor, neighborhood trying to reach our car. We started past a school and I said, "Not that way, it's horrible" for the playground was full of darting, dangerous, figures and there was a ghastly refuse-heap that smelled of carrion. So we walked another way and came past another schoolyard, this one full of "monkey bars" and slides and swings. Hundreds of vicious youths of both sexes were sitting on them. They spotted us and yelled "There go 3 of them!" and attacked us. I tried to reach the car but, seeing it was hopeless, stopped and picked up a wine bottle. I broke the bottle, making it into a weapon—jagged glass with the neck a stout handle. (The bottle was an empty half-gallon of Tivola—a good choice.) The largest, most vicious of them made a similar weapon (the street was full of empty bottles). I glanced at the others. My "brother" was lost in a swarm of them. My mother was handing them her purse, begging mercy. It was like being set upon by a troop of baboons . . .

I woke up and said, "Well, those are only thoughts. They may have come from something real, but now they are only thoughts. I can take them."

And I deliberately went back into the dream, over and over again (for that is something I have trained myself to do, seeing it as one of the skills of Poet). I met that viciousness over and over again, trying this way, and then that way—nothing worked.

I then woke fully, and began to weep. I have been weeping ever since. I cannot stop! (the grammar of that last sentence is not pity, but astonishment) I cannot *stop* ! (astonishment and despair)

I am struck by what is meant [by] "crying in the wilderness."

"Literally and in all senses" how wise Rimbaud was! (and that the *literally* part is what is most befogged—till we write down and down and down, as I have, almost getting to a plainness that obviates all poetry. Fighting the baboons again. As if to shatter that "more truth than poetry" vicious saying of all our vulgarity! And still to get ((from *Wobbly Rock*))!!!! the cry "I don't understand it.

53

Why don't you write so that everybody can understand it.?"

> It
> is
> a
> real
>
> rock

My God!!!

After the radiant vision of openness (which it will take me books to bring into words, for I thought at the time "no poetry, do not stop the flow of it (snagged in flight) but let it go through you"——and, incidentally, realized that that is what's wrong with wrong writing: it stops us, whereas Poetry means only "this is *flight*!!!! This is the open flow of it!!!")

After the radiant vision of openness, yesterday, I saw myself a ring of bone in a clear stream, and vowed never, ever, to close myself again.

But can I do it? Will it always hurt this much? What is it that hurts?

Shall I close myself a little while? Today? (I am eyeing the wine bottle again. I pour myself a cup of wine. I will rest.)

Will closing rest me?

What is it that hurts? What is it that needs resting?

(You do not have to answer this question. You cannot. That is precisely what *I* have to do.)

> And right now heard a
> "Ring of bone" with
> *Ring* as what a bell does

What does that mean?

• • • • • •

All that is left to say, here, is that this is the moment of suicide (or, in my phrase:

> The instant
> After it is made

I hope all who would be Poet read this poem (for now I realize this is a poem, a letter and a poem, for it is still a letter written by a Poet to a Poet, for he needed to speak, and couldn't if there weren't a Poet to speak to)

54

The other possibility, *the only other possibility*, is suicide.

I have long been struck by the long list of suicides by Poets of our time. Yesterday I read for the first time Mayakovsky's suicide note:

> As they say
> 'the incident is closed.'
> Love boat
> smashed against mores.
> I'm quits with life.
> No need itemizing
> mutual griefs
> woes
> offences.
> Good luck and good-bye.

This, and the suicide of Crane of Lindsay of Thomas (through his drink, as Malcolm Lowry went, drowning in his vomit) as Wieners almost went and is miraculously back with us, by means of his enormous strength, though he seems so frail, and there are hundreds more you know of, or can find, easily, if you look around

These suicides are but a part of the job of Poet!

For whatever it is that hurts. Whatever it is that needs to rest from time to time. Whatever it is that can be opened to the flow of it, or closed from pain.

This must be killed again and again!

The really tragic thing about the drownings and gunshots and the irreclaimable madnesses is this:

They, Poets all of them, missed the truth of it by a quarter of an inch.

You do not have to do it with a gun. You do not really do it with a gun.

Though, lately, I begin to wonder how many more times I can kill this thing. Is he always going to grow? Will he always be that same shape? There is some error to the way I keep doing it. Perhaps I try to come *back* from it, instead of resting on it, when I'm *through* with it, hanging there, as one would hang, poised, in the center of the earth, if the earth had a shaft through it, and you jumped down the shaft.

What a jump that would be! Is!

Up and down. Up and down. Through. Below. Above.

I am through with this.

I cannot stay as open as this.

I am going to be drunk the rest of this day. But only for the rest
of this day.

Closed.

DEAD!

. . . .

Robert, I have stopped weeping. I am buzzy, though not yet drunk. I went to the creek and washed my face, after first reading this that I wrote to you.

I thank God for this gift, as you must have, on many occasions. It has saved me again. As it must have saved you, again & again.

Is this why he keeps coming back again and again, to be killed?

Do you see how the writing goes! How it brings it all *up* at the end?

You, who have this gift, for you could not have this gift unless you often took trips as black as this, as painful

AND IT IS NOT NECESSARY!!!

(in theory at least)

Is Rimbaud's way the only way, in this vulgar age? That we must finally kill Poet out of our total contempt for this time that mocks us?

This letter was neither completed nor sent.

To Charles Olson, from Big Sur, 22? *July* 1962

Dear Charles,   Neither of us has written you for a long time, or perhaps ever, but now I have been staying at Lawrence Ferlin-ghetti's cabin for 11 days and haven't seen a soul in all that time, and now Lawrence has returned and I go elsewhere, and sitting here, reading from your *Maximus Poems,* I, reading your poems carefully again, giving them the care they deserve and always

reward, bringing to Lawrence certain passages he may have missed
—we would like simply to say hello Charles, it is a bad time, made
bearable by you and the men you celebrate in your beautiful book.

I thought this was going to be some kind of chain letter-type-
deal, but I see that Lawrence has a thick pen in hand and is writing
you that way. This gives me, somehow, more room to give my trib-
ute its wanted space.

Thank you. You have done more than even the high purpose of
showing us how "to go on." That is not just literary talk. I can't
help but be struck by that line—it moves so much freer, says what
it has to, strikes, out.

I have moved for 2 years now with the fishermen of the West
Coast—we of the beautiful boats, the Monterey "clippers" (yacht
owners named them that—what they really are are little boats
designed 300 years ago in Italy, so carefully made they never are
caulked and (I've seen this) do not take water though the keel was
made in 1918)—or the boats of the Nordskies, the double-enders
from Seattle.

We have trollers here, all the fish caught by hand, and the boats
run by one man only, or, at the most, two, and it is the same thing.
I can't make a living anymore. Even the boat owners (I get only
20%) will lose them and know it.

It is all over. You know it and I know it. I can't, here, tell you all
about West Coast fishing, the land which made me, as the coast
you MADE, stand, has made you. It is over. All of it.

And we do what we can. You do it perfectly.

Charles, it is just not possible to write any better than you do—
or from anything bigger.   Lew

FROM A POCKET NOTEBOOK, DATED 6 AUGUST 1962

Imagining
Equivalent of kiss
for Eagles

—

"Stay outside as much as I should" yet
Know the names (at 36) of, maybe,
4 or 15 kinds of bird, a
Few flowers ("They's

Roses
Lilies & thousands of
Hog
Wortle")

While almost
all the needled
Conebearers stand
Nameless beside my (fishing) streams . . .

This, which
Was deliberate, now is
Neglect—a laziness

The man who thinks
    he's got something
has lost the only
    thing he's got

Concern for minute things
gives scale to all this size
        tiny white flowers
blue ones with raindrops
        neatly placed on all 4 petals

_____

Snow water
10 miles of flowing over
        hot boulders
The waterfall is warm
        soap—shower—luxury

_____

Why do we dream of lost cities when
Lost groves grow beyond the next rock knoll
the next and next . . .

"Deer may safely graze"

And all that man is—
    which is all that
    sickens me—

Drops away again
   into the same old poem
You bear with me.

To Philip Whalen, from Larkspur, California, 17 *August* 1962

Dear Philip,   I am at Kirby Doyle's house right now & read in a letter from you to him that you wondered where I was (am).

I am now completely cured of all my foolishness, pain, despair, bitterness, the flinch is gone. My whole life is again reorganized, this time to me liking (for a while).

Now what I'm going to do is (read that in the voice of Miss Kids) go up to the Salmon River and live in a mining claim cabin & catch big steelhead and never see people & drink good spring water and not worry if the bomb goes off MEANWHILE writing all truth into imperishable pomes.

The Salmon River is located as per map. I have been all over this Western country and I've never seen a river more beautiful. I will spend my life there. You must come up and visit me as soon as possible. There is no rent to pay. I will write you as soon as I'm really set up with permissions & all the firewood cut. We can talk and eat fish.

I have been living all my life with half my mind as square & snobbish as F. Scott Fitz. It has been shown to me at last that I am only made miserable by that world & that a small amount of strength, discipline, clarity of purpose etc. (list here all the virtues Mr. Snyder seems to have quite naturally)—unless I move out of cities and stay off the juice I'll just be sick and miserable and frightened, and I guess I really don't want that tho you'd never know by just watching me operate most of the time.

So I now will have $100 (refund from insane effort to kill myself by buying expensive property in Big Sur—a story too shameful to tell you, here, tho I may tell it someday) & with that I can last till mid October when Momma will prolly be able to find another $100 etc. I don't worry *only* when I'm under big trees by a good fishing river, far from Scott's silly world (a world I was born to & except by a (I now know) *fortunate* accident would have been rich enough to do right—so there I'd be, rich, without genius, drunk, charming, powerful.

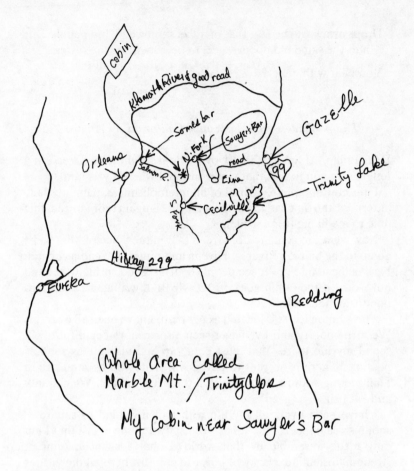

(Whole area called
Marble Mt. /Trinity Alps

My Cabin near Sawyer's Bar

As it is I suppose I'll have to be (as they say) the first "world poet" since Whitman and Lawrence. Won't that be fun? If that happens I promise to tell the whole world how much I am indebted to you for being around, more genius in yr. little finger than I have except 5 minutes out of every year (and then I'm usually too drunk to talk).

I hear you and Les are still worried about yr. house, rent, etc. That's too bad. Why don't you split from the city? I'll write you letters. Lots of people will. You won't be any lonelier than you are now & it costs less & you can take long walks in the real world. And then, every now and then, you can visit people & be the visiting lion & get fed and fondled (which people would rather do for a seldom visitor than for the man who lives down the street).

I am struck by the fact that of all us supposedly hip people only Ginsberg & Snyder & Corso seem to be outwitting the system. It is shameful. Don't you think so? Fuck it, I'M tired of all that.

I've been trying to read Creeley with pleasure & confess I cannot. What's all the fuss about? All I see is childish (or pot) rhymes & a streak of viciousness—a real power thing clothed better but as uninteresting as Spicer's: certainly none of Olson's or Williams' real size and love. I must be wrong—Duncan & Olson have this huge respect for his work & they are a lot smarter than I am.

Am WRITING again. Many new poems. Good ones. Very musical. I am accepting the Irish sounds, the pretty ones, like:

> Orange, the brilliant slugs,
> Nibbling at leaves of trillium

Isn't that pretty? And long poems written weeping. I accept my gift of tears.

I have been in a very bad way, Philip, but now it's all something else again and I like it now. I bought a good axe.

Tomorrow I will arise early and go to Big Sur and get my $100 back, then I'll return and visit you. If you have 3 pages of poems I know where you can place them for $25—or write 6 and get $50. A real offer. I'll tell you all about it when I see you. I intend to force 9 pages on them for $75. I will use the money for new boots and a Kelty pack. And whiskey.   always your loving nephew   Lew

"Miss Kids": Joanne Kyger.

To Gary Snyder and Joanne Kyger, from Forks of Salmon, California, 10 September 1962

Dear Gary & J. Eliz.   Here I am sitting in the woods with my typewriter on top of my footlocker & my legs all cramped up monk style, after the manner you taught me, writing you this letter way across the ocean. I have 2 tailor-made cigarettes left.

That poor miserable fellow who used my name and body all last winter finally went off to pout or mope somewhere else. I hope he never comes back, but he probably will—just when everything gets set to my liking.

Right now I am free to get down to business again & am hanging around here trying to beg a cabin for the winter. It looks like I'll succeed, tho maybe it'll be a very cold little log affair owned by a strange paranoid right out of Faulkner ("stamped out of tin" as per "Barn Burning"—the first emergence of a Snopes).

"Here" is on the Salmon River in Trinity Alps/Marble Mt. area —the best river I've ever seen & I've seen a lot of rivers. Each day I catch a fish (now salmon, later steelhead) abt. 7 to 10 lbs. & I eat him all day. With potatoes for dinner, with Cream-of-Wheat for breakfast, cold for lunch. I always fart a great deal when I eat salmon.

Everything blew up. I ain't no commercial fisherman. There's no fish and the boats are cold and cramped. I work, but I don't get paid, and I get very bitter. I got so bitter & ugly even Lenore gave me up & she's most patient. Then I went to Big Sur and *really* flipped. But good—someday you'll see the poems about it. The thing is that this culture thinks it's only a sickness, that you only need to be calmed or "cured" (like bacon?) & thereby the only means of spiritual opening, growth, is denied us & we all sit around nervous and bland.

So once again I've changed my entire life & will never leave this place again, and never live in cities. I said this 3 years ago & chickened out. But at that time I'd never really known the love of a true woman & was short that measure of necessary strength. Now I do know what that is, how big & good it can be, and am able, as Wittgenstein sd. to "go on." It was very good. No complaints. I will watch for it to happen again. And again.

But the old hang-up, the longing for a home, a place to put the typewriter & plant trees, is still crowding my life. Will I ever solve it? So many I know get nested in real nice for long periods, strew their stuff around, invite people over. But the old image of myself persists: the figure of a Prince without land or power, borrowing a corner of somebody else's estate. I've decided to admit this image, meet it head on, smash it somehow—seeing it as tangled up with all I know. It is there, I must deal with it. It is not "neurotic," but is archetypical, can stand, if I work at it honestly enough, as strongly as Whitman's "where shall we sleep tonight?" (which in his speech is a boom of freedom). What I'm saying is, I get my steam from this longing, however ignorant it may be & it does no good to say "look man, you've got your campsite, that, now, is 'home.'" It is not! I will not pretend I understand something which is so deep in the fogs of me no verbal proof counts. Until I can know what other men know when they say "this is where I live," I will know nothing of worth—and when I can say that & feel it deeply, I'll know most of what I'll ever be able to know. "This is where I live." What a thing to know!

There is a claim here on the Salmon I could buy for only $500. Ten acres with a spring, huge cedars, enough gold to pay my way (together with the sale of a few stories). Symbolically, it's eerily (sp?) perfect: name "Jughead Mine," location *other side of the river*, also named for a cat, part Siamese & part bobcat (I was going to call it Krazy Kat, because it *is* that, until I found its more accurate real same name—isn't that odd?). When I was first on it I asked the shade of my grandfather the first question I ever asked him. He sent me affirmative tears.

But who has $500? What matter if it's ridiculously priced (worse places are going for $2,500)? I can't go into debt, won't, even if, which they won't, anybody would loan me the money. That is part of it, part of the "way" it has to be.

It is now held by one of the sweetest couples I've ever met. He has one eye & the Forestry found out about that & took him off standby which, with the little gold he finds has been getting him through. And then they had a baby, after 10 years of marriage, & it turned out to be a Caesarean birth with a $750 price tag & the poor babies haven't any food for the winter. A real tough Polock named Novak who's been systematically bilked by this 'nation of finks.'

This winter Novak will teach me mining & I'll put all my poems together into one giant book (now titled "Earthbook") & generally get back to work.

Is Don Allen still in Kyoto? I'll write him tomorrow c/o you. Show him this letter so I won't have to repeat myself. What are you up to now? What news from Allen [Ginsberg]? Did they find that monsoon to stand naked in the jungle in? I & the whole world wait breathlessly to know. Apologies for all letters written prior to this & after abt. August. It is nice to be back.   Lew

To Philip Whalen and Leslie Thompson, from Forks of Salmon,
12 September 1962

Greetings Gentlemen,   Here I am in a beautiful forest where I have salmon and eggs every morning for breakfast. The fish run 5 to 10 pounds & the largest I caught took 35 minutes to land. I catch one each evening. It takes about a half hour.

I still haven't found a cabin for the winter, but have 4 possibilities (the owners are hard to pin down or find or both), and can rent one of 2 for maybe $15, so am not worried.

This is gorgeous country. I am camped on the river about ½ mile from the road & 2 miles from anybody. I goof. I have met dozens of very straight people & can buy a claim from one of them for $500 (but where do you find that?). They are very poor & I worry about them. Their land is worth abut 3,000 but they need a grubstake for the winter. New baybe & all that, debts, etc. It is a beautiful piece of land, 10 acres, with spring and gold & fish. I'll try.

What news? Nobody writes me letters & I go every day to P.O.

This mainly to give you my address and to ask if we're at war with any or all our enemies yet.

I'll invite you all up here if and when I have a place to invite you to. Steelhead soon. Deer season soon. Woods full of drunk people with big guns. Ugh.

I am all right now. Nobody believes I really cracked up, bad, but I'll say anyway it's all over. What a relief.

I'll never, ever, go back there again. You guys get out. It's bad.
Lew

To Kirby and Dee Doyle, from Forks of Salmon,
19 September 1962

My very most dear Mr. & Mrs. McSwine,   I am typing this in the failing light of evening on a board I cleverly nailed to a tree & tree stump. Soon I will light my kerosene lamp & carry on.

Everything is lovely. I have met dozens (actually 4) real nice people & I've even been finding work! There is more work for the likes of me here in the woods than ever in the city. Today I helped a man build his cabin. He is an old man, vile tongued & somewhat dirty (but we all are. It is mostly just dust & sweat). He pays me $2 the hour & feeds me huge stews. He worries bout me. Fine. I need all the help I can get.

No cabin yet, but spooky flukes. I keep just missing good deals by a few days, or because somebody sold some property & the buyer needs a place for the winter. I don't know whether to interpret this as meaning I shouldn't be here, or as a sign that something really great is in the offing & I am being (as they say) "brought along slow." I knew a kid who was brought along too fast, and he was a drooling idiot at age 40, and had been since he was 15 when, big, he was put into the ring with people as fierce & cagey as Archie Moore. I am, I decide, being toughened. The smart boys are watching. Soon I get a crack at the garden. It is Malcolm Lowry's garden. It has that sign on it. You know: "You like this garden? Why is it yours?" etc.

I certainly do like it. I improve all of it I touch. Picking up tin cans, burying toilet paper (smeared), building beautiful fireplaces — placing the rocks, Inca style, without mortar, so solidly they will last a thousand years. They are all perfectly level. I put the grills I got off you neatly in place & I have a cooking scene better than any stove.

Still, I goofed the first week. Forgot to drown my fire & the Forestry found out. Very embarrassing. Citation etc. The green fuzz hunting me out, & me still paranoid from cities. 2 days ruined. But I went & threw myself on the mercy of the District Ranger & he was very nice. Said it was, lately, experienced campers, he didn't know why. Dug my beat-up old G.I. equipment. Owned he knew I knew better. Laughed. Said, "Well, I guess you'll never do that again." And now I'm on "Standby" in case there's a forest fire. You should see how wet my fireplace is now every time I leave camp.

But the most exciting news is I found a real paradise I am going to buy. 10 acres of a mining claim for $500. A sweet spring. Cedar trees. Other trees, thousands of them. Gold (like, $200 a year if I work real hard for 3 months & am lucky, but enough gold to, under the law, hold the land). And dig: the name of the mine is "Jughead Mine." I was going to call it "Krazy Kat" till I learned its real name. Because it's like that. And then it turns out that "Jughead" is the name of a cat (half Siamese & half wild bobcat or something—a real far-out cat). So something is working there. Also, it is *on the other side of the river*! It is the most beautiful, difficult, crazy claim on this wild river. And I'm going to buy!

Now, this is how I'm going to try to pay for it. Momma agreed to give me $100 each month from October to October. I have lived here nearly 4 weeks & have spent 25 dollars. I have lived beautifully. Under the stars. Salmon & eggs each morning for breakfast. Nobody bugging me. Sanity returning. Long hikes. Good wind again. Etc. So, I am going to give 50 of my 100 every month to the present claim holder. Who is:

Pete & Sally Novak, at least the straightest people I've met in years. Portrait sketches too difficult at this time. Suffice it [to] say

65

they just had an unexpected baby after 10 years of marriage & don't have enough to eat this winter & are worried, especially because the baby was a Caesarean birth (she being green at the game) & it cost them $750. They are worried about me, too. I need all the help I can get.

But I worry about them. They would rather have $500 cash so they can get $750 worth of grub at special discount in Medford, Ore. (no tax & crazy deals to miner types etc.). He is a very tough, one-eyed Slav who is used to thinking in terms of winter grubstake. The $50 a month shot terrifies him. Sally, on the other hand, is a New York Jewish lady who placates, so beautifully, him. A love match! Way out here in the woods! Naturally. (all ways)

So babies, it is beautiful! I catch 5 or 10 pound salmon and eat him every day. Soon the steelhead run. Deer season starts the 20th & I have six or a dozen places all picked out. Also found a bear wallow.

I can build a log cabin on my claim for total money cost maybe $100. I've got it down now so all I need is windows, used at Cleveland [Wrecking Yard]?, and roofing paper 'cause I don't want to cut down 150 foot cedar I have for shakes (and you need big trees for heartwood).

God I wish somebody would fling me 5 bills so I could feed the Novaks & make my home! But who can do that? I'm a skinny Whitman: "Hello my angel, are you my banker?"

Instead, I will scratch it out. The Novaks will worry. And I might fail.

Meanwhile, I promised you a camping trip. If you have the time, come join me a while. All you need is sleepy bags & food money. We can arrange where I can meet you. With luck most of October will still be good. After that we'll make it a spring shot. You really ought to keep making that long bread until winter grubstake is put away.

I have a pint of ten-high here and I can't hardly type no more.

Less specifically, & for broader reasons, I am so full of love I can only think of sharing what I have, what I know (how to do). I am good in this country.

I'll never go back.   Lew

To Charles Olson, from Forks of Salmon, 26 September 1962

Charles,   Somehow this letter never got mailed & here I find it in my duffle.

I have finally taken to the woods. I hope forever. They very nearly wiped me out this last time. One keeps thinking he ought to know better, be tougher, wiser, or something. But I, at least, just cannot be at my work, which I see as a matter of opening, if I place myself too near the center of that vulgar and dangerous din. One closes, must close, for survival & is defeated.

Here I can keep my eyes open all the way, all day long, and never have that or any other sense appalled (no dictionary, can't spell). I see this absolutely literally—with sound, for example, as a matter of too many decibels. You just stop hearing if you ride a subway often enough. It is a giant insult to the senses, the sense. One's whole being *must*, at least mine must, withdraw.

It is, by trail ony, 4½ miles & 2,000 feet down to the road where the mailbox is. I will describe it all, am describing it, am getting it all down. Meanwhile, I'd deeply enjoy hearing from you.   Lew Welch

"this letter never got mailed": the letter to Charles Olson of 22? July 1962.

To Lew Welch, from Gary Snyder, 31 Nishinomiya-cho, Kita Ku, Kyoto, 11 October 1962

Dear Lew   Can there really be such a place as Forks of Salmon? I hope you are still where you were when you wrote me. With a cabin come through, & a bunk & a woodstove or fireplace & then you can have some friends over, just like you say.

New notes on thought: (to tack onto Lao-tzu or Wittgenstein)
    a. that which is not understood cannot be expressed
    b. to be fully understood it must be expressed.
    c. there is no "inexpressible"   the problem is understanding
    So, actually, ideally, he who speaks knows. he who doesn't speak doesn't know.

How to get along easy: get some instant oatmeal. Add a lot of raisins. chop up some dried apricots, peaches, figs, whatever, as fine as you have patience. Add to above, along with busted up peanuts & almonds & ground nuts, tochews, pecans, etc. natural nuts

67

& dates, if you can afford any. Put in lots of wheat germ, toasted is best. Mix in a bit of soy flour if there is any, and also a spoonful or two of brewer's yeast if you don't mind the flavor. Put in lots of brown sugar and powdered milk. Put it all in a bag or can. Now you can eat this any time by adding cold or hot water and letting it soak one minute. It will serve as all purpose food, and is great for quick mountain or poetry writing breakfast lunch & dinner. Better than sandwich for you.

There is a funny bunch in Brookville Ohio publishing a magazine called *Way Out* & advocating Homestead Movement—Green Revolution (return to wild soil) American Individualist Anarchism —anti Usury a la Pound—Confucian Vegetarian Sexual & Agricultural Cummunism. Plan is to get individuals or groups around the country to move into cheap-soil isolated farming & wilderness districts, "homesteading." write Robert Anton Wilson above address c/o magazine for gassy literature. They sent it me via Ginsberg's recommendation. Trouble is they're all city folks I suspect.

How to have a Tibetan style robe: take any old bathrobe of heavy wool. cut off the belt loops and pockets. Fix a button on the right side somewhere so you can sort of close it if it's cold. Dye it deep red or brown. Get a long sash, or dye the same sash with it. Tie the sash low around the waist. When you have to run or work, pull up the robe & let it lap down over the sash, you can pull it up as far as you like. Put lunch or small animals or books inside the robe in back over the sash. let it down again when you lie down or sit crosslegged.

Another suggestion: try eating big trout or salmon raw. It's wonderful. slice it cross-grain about half-inch slices. Dip it in sauce made of horseradish mixed with soy sauce.

Another thing: if you stay there this winter be sure and wear long underwear, the warmest you can get, all the time. & put a sweater over your T shirt UNDER your shirt. Then you'll be warm.

Tell me what I can do for you.

Next time I don't think I'll be so didactic. WRITE us soon   love, Gary

[P.S.] Dear Lewis   I don't have *no* advice. I like chocolate.   Love, Eliz.

[On back of air letter:] Nota bene: the Tibetan style robe as described within is worn by Tibetans like a coat over ordinary clothes

To Gary Snyder, from Forks of Salmon, 11 *October* 1962

Dear Gary,   I am writing this letter while seated at a desk I built in an old shack cabin (shake-cabin, I meant) 3½ miles, by trail only, and 2,000 feet above the road where the mailbox is. It is where I live.

Supernatural events led me gradually to this place—a place of such beauty, dignity, and fine history I am humbled, finally, right back into my total mind & will never again be bitter and complaining and afraid.

You cross the river at a rickety old bridge the Forestry engineers put up (I'm told) by mistake, it should have been 3 miles further up the river, and proceed along a jeep road for about a mile and a half until you come to a big flat. There you cross the creek and begin climbing up an impossible switchback trail. 2 miles later you arrive at a mountain meadow with a lake in it & this fine old shake cabin sitting all by itself. Virgin forest is all about the place—the trees all over 100 feet high and practically no underbrush.

I found this place, as I say, by easing along with spooky hints that zeroed me into it as directly as they could. First, I investigated the curious rickety bridge that led nowhere. I found a beautiful piece of land, unclaimed, with a bear wallow on it & a dead bear lying beside it. I spent 2 days roaming around on it, and was finally discouraged by surveyor stakes all over the place. I then got a job helping an old man build his cabin, & with the money I bought new boots. I moved the old man from Yreka & returned to this forest to discover there was a big forest fire. The Asst. Ranger came by in a truck 10 minutes after I got to the old man's place. I hailed him, and got hired to fight the fire. "Take the next truck" he said. The next truck was full of 4 engineers headed by one of the coolest bureaucracy manipulators I've ever seen—a guy who knows his way around!

Happy that I had new boots to fight the fire with (my old ones were flapping at the soles and were torn at the sides), I eased along with the cool group & got 3 full 16 hour days out of the fire—the last two spent sleeping by a campfire & taking a walk looking for smoldering stumps, maybe every 4 hours. I got more time in than any other "pick up." Made $94.

But best of all, learned that these very engineers were the guys who put the surveyor stakes up! Also, they spent last winter in this cabin & told me how to get here. Also, they told me no one owns it or has claimed it. Also, they informed me that a road will come within 100 feet of the place within 2 years (and the new road won't use that crazy bridge either).

It turns out that the first place I was interested in is right on the road, and I'm going to claim it and build a shed on it to use as my supply depot for the 2 years before the road goes in.

A week before all this I was given a fruit salad by people in the camp next to me, and during the conversation we had when I returned their bowl, they directed me to a beautiful little valley full of yew trees. This valley turns out to be only one mile from here on another approaching trail.

Then, I decided to use the other trail (for complicated reasons) the first time I brought gear up here. (I had already taken the engineers' directions and found the place, wept when I saw it . . .)

I lost my way, fell, and while trying to disentangle myself, let my pack roll down hill and I couldn't find it! Spent all day hunting for it & returned defeated, confused, ashamed. Imagine losing your pack! So the next day I went back to find it and ran into (very strangely, I won't go into it all now) an 80 year old man hunting way up on this high ridge above my lost pack. I told him what I was doing, where I was going, etc., and we had a long talk, during which he told me the guy who built this place never claimed it. He was a Wobbly! He wouldn't do one damned thing to aid the finks! "I'm going to move in, maybe" I said, departing. "Drain the lake," he says, "you get a beautiful garden that way" says the old man—a tough old Indian I learned later. (By the way, his wife, old as he is probably, was hunting with him—"She's up there on the ridge somewhere" . . .)

Finally, just before all this, I lost a cabin I had all set up—and by very curious circumstances. Lost 2 places, in fact. I became convinced at that time (even through my paranoia) that something was up, that I was being saved for something better.

I have left no event out. *Every* sign pointed right to this place, many of them, as you can see, long before I knew there was anything here. I am sure the shade of the old Wobbly put me here to keep the place up. [. . .]

I have new boots & a chain saw (a beautiful little McCulloch I bought with my fire money . . . still owe a few $$) and just enough money from home to keep me in eats. This will be the first time in my life I've had (1) enough money, and (2) enough strength, and (3) a place of my own. I am still jumpy about it. Got Jean Greensfelder's .22 and will shoot any fink who says I gotta move.

It has rained for 4 days & my car is parked on that bad jeep road. The roof has not leaked one drop. I got plenty firewood (22 big sections all bucked out by Forestry for surveyors last winter—one cord wood already chopped by them, I chopped 2 more—2 double bit axes found in woods, one Kelly, one Collins, both brand new—bit wedges & sledge—good stove. They's even glass in all the windows! Doors of hand-hewn oak. Will soon send photos.

In next letter, Gary, will tell you of beautiful plan which includes you & J. Eliz. when (if) you ever get back. Right now must quit this and tinker with my house, set rat traps, empty piss cans. I've learned to piss a full 2 pound coffee can every night. Isn't that astonishing?

If Don Allen still there show this to him, tell him I'll write real soon. I want him to know I'm finally set up and will write all those books he keeps saying I ought to. Nothing would please me more than to have you and him & J. Eliz here right now to enjoy this beautiful rain. My lake, intermittent, nearly empty when I got here, is full. Lew

[P.S.] first letter from Rat Flat, October 11, 1962—actual registered name of place—small collection of pomes coming up: "Songs in Rat Flat" address, however, still Forks of Salmon, California

To Kirby Doyle, from Forks of Salmon, 11 October 1962

Kirby, I have news to tell more strange than that of all Fables, i.e. fabulous. First, however, let's exorcise your ghosts.

You were too harsh with Kerouac, and you know it, hence the guilt. There is far more to him than rummy and therefore numb lover, there is that truth-seeker which is all of us who try for more than comfort (as far as I can see the only goal of fat fink 'Murca). And naturally you find fault with his writing as we all must find fault with the writing of others, since we are on our own, "in the open" as Olson says, making our own shape, shoving our "shoulder" (as Mike says) into a blank blank, that something never seen before shall remain forever there, like a boulder in the living room (my phrase). And we are so caught up in, dedicated to, our own part seen vision and scarcely sketched out work, that we are "confused" (Stein's word) by the closeness, but not right, of shape coming out of others of our time, and we cannot read our fathers either as

71

Stein says, for the closeness, so read Whitman and Thoreau and Rabelais, not Williams, for it is clear when we read our grand-fathers, but confusing with fathers or brothers because of closeness. It is a problem of tuning.

I have seen Whalen so caught in all this that he was criticizing someone, maybe Faulkner or Lowry, and someone said why and he said "Real books are entirely different" and they said, what is a real book, and he, honest to God, blocked up cold and couldn't name a real book or a right author from EVER! What it was was his own vision of what he will do, but hasn't quite. And they will certainly be some books as we all know.

And you know all this, and you know I know it, so when you come on salty about one of the few of us who is getting any work done, you have bad dreams. And if I am the avenging angel in these dreams I am glad, because it shows you know you can't shuck me any more than I can shuck you (as was shown so well by the won't-loan-car incident).

You have bad dreams when you write out of your fear and bit-terness & you grow strong when you write out the bottom humble-ness and love that is the gravel ('cause you ain't hit bedrock yet), you've got to [be] digging away at it with borrowed tools, and then invented tools, all the while shoring it up with standards of honesty wrung out of you like tears.

So naturally everybody looks like a phony only they aren't, as you know.

there.

. . . .

Now what *I* wanted to say is (in voice of J. Eliz.):

only this sentence is in that voice, the rest must not be, I am trying to find a transition, I stop, must stop to drink tea. What I have to tell is really big news (voice of Ed Sullivan) shit!

(NEW LETTER ENTIRELY   )

VOICE FROM RAT FLAT!

Supernatural Events Lead
Bard to Mountain Paradise

"Agony over?"
Weeps Poet

Dear Kirby,   This letter should be the telling of the whole story, which is more than a book. It is one I will write this winter: "A Place to Put the Typewriter."

But here I can only tell you what I've found, at so long last, leaving out the years of being cursed by homelessness—that I very nearly gave up before coming here, that I cracked as you saw. And that the reason, the deep basis, has always been my vision of myself as the intruder, the sometime visitor, the poacher on another's estate, the Prince without land. I have had no place to stand, no footing to swing my axe from. I have never had a home. I have never had a place to put the typewriter. I have had to snatch time to sketch out little parts of what I see, scribbling on envelopes, typing on boxes, picnic tables, office typewriters, and though Lenore made a beautiful home for me out of nothing, that nothing, the little we needed and I couldn't give, drove me to stunned silence. All that I have to leave out.

I have a home. It is so beautiful I still weep every time I stop doing whatever and just look at it. It is mine by law for life, if I do the few small things I need to do to hold it. It was given to me by the ghost of an old Wobbly, who built it—and the events that led me here are so strange I will have to remake my entire picture of the Universe to fit them in.

You cross the Salmon River at a rickety old bridge that leads nowhere. I'm told it was put there, by inconceivable error, several years ago, when the Forestry engineers missed the proper site by about 3 miles. You go a mile and a half on an old jeep road, then leave the road and drive across a field (a "flat" in local lingo, so named out of contrast to these terrific steep gorges). Then you cross a large creek, by tight-roping it across some fallen alders, and you come to a steep, switchbacking trail. The trail goes only up. There is no relief until the very top where you come to a mountain meadow with an intermittent lake in it and a beautiful old shake cabin surrounded by virgin forest—the trees over 100 feet high, moss grown, and almost all the underbrush killed by shade.

A shake cabin is made by nailing big cedar shingles over a frame of poles made from 3 to 6 inch diameter pine trees. This one was made by a craftsman such as the world will probably never see again. The doors and window frames are made of oak planks apparently split, not sawn, from native oak. It has rained continuously for 5 days & not one drop has leaked in. The inside is all golden with the natural woods, and crisscrossed with delicate bracing. It is like living in a Vermeer.

The man who built it, Lawrence Meyer, never claimed it, located it, or registered it. I call him "Wrench" because of following half-sign he cut into a board (now part of shelving)

MILE CABIN
HISLERS ALLOWED
WRENCE MEYER

He just squatted on it, a Wobbly who paid no taxes, would in no way recognize the government. They were chiselers to him as they're finks to us. He died, I am told, 5 or more years ago. From other signs I know he called the place "100 mile cabin," as it was, from Eureka, with no roads in until the 30s. Everything here was brought in by mule or built from the forest. He has a quartz mine somewhere, I haven't found it yet. But I know 2 people, both of them Indians, who know where it is if it should escape me. I have to find the mind in order to hold this place (notice type "mind" for "mine"?), because I have claimed it & must do token mining to hold it. Or I may lease it for 99 years (at about $40 per year). I would like to squat as he did, but am not as tough as he was, and I believe our times to be even more dangerous than his. And it was pretty dangerous in his day—they castrated, hung, and burned a Wobbly in Everett, Washington. [. . .]

I just went to the privy to shit. The smoke from my fire drifts low, pushed down by rain, over the lake. The wind is making a strange sound—like angry bees. These trees are so high, no wind ever gets to the cabin.

· · · · · · ·

As I said in the headline, supernatural events lead me here. *Every* occurrence for more than 2 weeks has pointed me up here, many of them occurring before I, or the people involved, or the reasons involved, had any knowledge that this place even existed.

First, I was curious about that crazy bridge that leads nowhere. Here is this big steel bridge over the Salmon River and nothing is on the other side. Just this little jeep road & 2 houses to be sure, but they had a tram on a cable, as many "other side" places around here do. Nosing around, I found a beautiful piece of land I intended to claim, with idea of future building site. However, there were surveyor stakes all over it & I gave up, believing it to be already claimed (as most every inch of this country is).

Then I got a job helping an old man build his cabin. I then helped him move his stuff from Yreka, and on the very day I returned I learned there was a big forest fire. 10 minutes after arriving at the old man's, the assistant ranger came by in a truck, I hailed him and got hired to fight the fire. "Take the next truck" he says. The next truck turned out to have 4 surveyors in it, the very ones who put the stakes up, and they had spent the previous winter in this cabin! The leader was a real Bilko who got me all the soft duties & I ended up with 46 hours work—the longest of any "pick up." I made $94.

(Altogether, after so much working for no pay in S.F., I was here 3 weeks, worked 7 days, and made $120 and an almost new Coleman lamp.)

Before this, a party next to me, camping, gave me some fruit salad and during the conversation following my returning of the bowl they told me of a beautiful valley full of yew trees. It turns out to be only 1/2 a mile or so from here to another approaching trail.

Then, while coming into the place with gear for the first time I foolishly tried to make a new trail (the Yew Valley trail), got lost, fell, and while trying to disentangle myself, let my pack roll down into a deep canyon. I lost it! I looked all day for it and couldn't find it, and returned, shamed, defeated, confused. By this time I could smell the omens, so knew there must have been a reason. The next day, returning to get my pack, I did everything I could to avoid the area some hunters might be in (seeing their car & not wanting to get shot at) and ran smack into one on a very improbable trail. It was a Mr. Stanshaw, 80 year old man mostly Indian, hunting above lost-pack-gorge (with his wife! incidently). He knew Meyer and filled me in on all the details. I'm sure he'll prove to be a very valuable source of information & a good friend. Found the pack immediately and came in.

Altogether then, I slowly circled on this place, blind, led by *every* event (o yes, one more important one: had a nice cabin promised, definitely, and lost it by very spooky circumstances—owner helpless and very sorry. It was at that moment I deliberately eased off, feeling sure I was being saved for something better, as I told you in my last letter. By easing off I mean getting into that overdrive you use gambling or whenever in need of floating in on destiny etc.—of course the way to live always but who can?).

Finally, all this jelled the *day* of the big rains. I've been tooling up that horrible trail between showers, just got enough food and wood and bedding and cook pans in, and it has poured continuously for 5 days. Before this just camping, floating, without even a tent. Unless it happened exactly *when* it did, I was in pretty bad shape.

That, kiddies, is the end of the ghost story. Wrench and I are very happy it all worked out so sweetly. I shall save his house. The floor is rotten and in a few years it would have fallen down. And who around here has the love it needs? Or knows what a Wobbly is? Or cares about diddly shit?

BUDDHIST BARD TURNS
RAT-SLAYER

"Kill, kill, kill"
Shrieks Word-Smith

Horrible infestation of rats. Rats scampering over face, clawing at old shakes, nervously scuttling like mad things. No sleep at all for 2 nights. I went mad one night, leaped out of the sleeping bag and pounded the walls. My only light, a kerosene barn lantern, showed many little faces staring down at me from the rafters: not frightened, bemused at my antics. By this time I had dozens of little sardine cans filled with poison-pellets. "Eat! Eat!" I screamed, vowing traps, guns, unspeakable tortures. Then I went after one with a hammer and broke the handle.

Now all of them are dead, the last one trapped, all the rest poisoned. And I miss them!! They were mountain pack rats, gray with snow-white bellies and white feet. They collect everything. In the enormous nests I found after tearing out the canvas ceiling I found shaving brushes, toothbrushes, .22 cartridges, pencils, and a small calendar I am now using.

The canvas ceiling is now spread neatly out over the side of the little knoll the cabin sits on. The rain has washed it clean as the sails on a storm-beaten sloop. Last night something, perhaps a bear, nuzzled it all up into a heap. I took this as a sign that it was time to turn it over and wash the other side. Did so. The rafters are so pretty I hate to put the ceiling up again, but I think I'll have to after it turns cold (now it's 50 to 60, about like S.F.). Will take pictures before I put it back up (I've asked that the family camera be mailed here, will take many shots, details of doors, rafters, cabin in setting of great trees, etc.).

• • • • • • • •

That's the news, Kirby, except for one very important thing, the

76

thing that makes it all into a Grand Coup: within 2 years that road the boys were surveying will come within 100 feet of my door. No one knew that! There I'll be, turning on on my porch, while armies of bulldozers push my road to my door! Meanwhile, that other bit of land is, it turns out, unclaimed. I intend to claim it and build a small shed as a supply depot during the 2 years I have to play mule.

Get yourself some good boots—ones that lace up, the hood boots will only get you a turned ankle—and a sleeping bag. I have an extra cot, eats, everything. October is mild here, usually, and after this rain the woods will be beautiful. Even now the dogwood is coming on with lavender leaves. If you can make it, please do. I could use a little help putting this ceiling back in & other 2 man jobs. I promise not to make you pack huge loads up this terrible trail. Without pack it's puffy, but not bad. Plan to stay at least a week. We can meet in Yreka. I really want you to see this place. NRA boxes! Many curios! Deer drinking by the lake.

Please see that Mike, Phil, the folks at Auerhahn, Jay Blaise, Albert, Lenore, the East-West House, the Greensfelders. . .I see the list is impossible. What I want is that many people get this news and I can't see writing this long long letter over and over again. Why don't you just take from page 2 on (the first shall be private instruction) and leave it at Auerhahn Press. I'll tell everyone it's there.

What I really ought to do is mimeo it—I can think of 25 people who must know! Maybe I'll start a small mimeo newsletter: RAT FLAT VOICE. Do you think people would pay $1 a year? I'd send it 1st class so as to avoid all trouble like *floaty bear* had, case I want to talk dirty.

I have legally named this place Rat Flat. Intend a small collection of poems: "Songs in Rat Flat."

So here I am in my new boots, 3½ miles, by trail only, and 2,000 feet above the road where the mailbox is, thinking of you.

(and since this may be read by you all . . . . all my friends   Lew [P.S.] address: Forks of Salmon, California
IMPORTANT!!! (note: please *do not* use "Rat Flat" as address. Claims are filed by name & I don't want people nosing into my business at the Recorder's office. This is important. I may be slow meeting mining requirements & could lose this place by default if wrong people see records.

NO AID TO FINKS!

Diane di Prima published "New Letter Entirely" in *Floating Bear* #25, 1962.

To Joanne Kyger, from Forks of Salmon, 1 *November* 1962

Dear J. Eliz, Won't those Jap postmen have fun with that address, & everything? They'll prolly think we always do it that way and will take on a huge movement of hyphenated names but they won't sound german & hip & have all those Y's.

Which is why I write this letter: you are so wise. Yes, I promise not to make it so *good* it will seem real *bad* later. Already, I am *not* living in that beautiful cabin because the hike is so horrible & I got a real plain (ugly, even) little cabin right by the river with no hiking & tho I dream of Rat Flat & see it as the right place for a tormented poet to live I admit I just can't keep making that terrible hike 2 miles STRAIGHT UP! O.K.?

Everything is so beautiful I ought to be, as they say, "swinging" all the time but mostly I am nicely melancholy, just like that blind son-of-a-bitch said we ought to be.

I lost a real good girl there, J.E., and all because I'm such a flippy tormented type & will never learn to love anybody except in general. However, I am very good at loving people, in general, and will no doubt end up rich & famous as Whitman. There's a Saving & Loan Bank in Long Island named after *him*, so it just goes to show you what the rewards are if a fellow keeps plugging along.

As for the chocolates, you have no idea how delighted I was to have somebody *finally* ask *me* for something. Everyone has been so nice to me lately & I smile and take what they give saying "Thank you, I need all the help I can get." And I really did need it, I was in very bad shape. But now I am not in bad shape & you asked for chocolates & I was so pleased. But there aren't any chocolates here. I looked under the fir trees. I looked in the rancid lake. I looked in the nests of the pack rats. No chocolates.

I found a very funny fungus. It's almost too big to ship & you can't eat it it's so woody. But it's yours if you want it.

I have that picture of you which came in the last letter pinned on my wall. (add *that* sentence to yr. collection!) Do you really *know* how you are now even more beautiful then you ever were? In such a different way? Nex time I kiss you onna titty, Lew

78

Dear Gary,   Elevation 3200, trees around are doug fir & sugar pine & yew. Many small oaks & maples. Dogwood. Dogwood now lavender. Everything else fantastic unpaintable yellow and evergreen. Yes, found pack 18 feet from one of my blazes—I was certainly denied finding it until I had met Stanshaw (the old hunter next day). Yr. reading of half-sign exact as I figured you'd be. Indians here are Hupa, powerful 5'5" types with very handsome faces, very dark, almost black, skin, smoke gray eyes when mixed (as most are). Big family Bennett, the old owners of practically all this country. They married Indians. Present Bennetts everywhere. Main family has swede blood in them & strongest Bennett is 6'2 weighs 230 is called (only by very respected friends) "big swede." His features, color, entirely Hupa. Homer, his brother, is postman, good friend of Dan Wann (see below) & has Jap machine-gun bullet metal still in both legs. "I still can't like those people" he says. Who can blame him? Homer best hunter, tracker, trapper, in area. Wonderful guy. Not huge like brother. I think he may get to like me a little. I made mistake of coming on pacifist during recent Cuban business & didn't have time to really explain myself. Plan to at first chance—I really love these people & don't want to queer myself for imagined political or cowardly reasons. They can only read such a position as cowardly, tho Dan Wann, I think, understands or wants to.

Dan Wann is a big man, 70 years old, with white beard & 357 pistol nearly always at side. Generous, easy, tough as real big men are —nothing to prove. I came off my mountain to learn "Dan Wann owns that cabin, you can't live there." Went to see him, told him my story, and he says "No, I don't own that cabin, nobody does, ol' boy built it sells me everything in it & goes to Sacramento and dies. But I got something better if you want a quiet place to write." And he sets me up in Wrench Meyer's last house: a tiny cabin of CCC sections with ceiling 6'2" high. I guess the poor guy was tired of being cold at 100 mile cabin. He was over 80 when he turned his apron in.

So the spooky thing continues. I am here in Wrench's last house, living across the river from his best friend. It even looks like I'll end up with his rifle, an old 25-35 now owned by Dan Wann's son.

That hike is too much for me now & the snow gets 6 feet deep in winter and worse, the water is horrible—tastes like copper. I was looking for a spring. Wrench was a miner, never bothered, I'm sure I'll find one. Plenty of good pipe up there in case I find one far away. I will move to Rat Flat in spring. Now must continue healing process, write, rest, get fat on venison.

Thanks for all the advice. Haven't made up jiffy-o.k.-beat-ground-nuts-Zen hiking food, but will. Have long undies. Will work with saw as faller's helper on fires, $5 hour, until good enough to fall burning trees myself. Figure 5 to 7 hundred a summer that way. Lookouts all going to women now. Trail crew such miserable work. Dan is going to teach me how to find pockets of gold, intend to spend at least 1 maybe 2 months a year "sleeping on the rocks" as they say here. This country really wild, steep, nobody around. Too tough, altogether, for tourists, even very tough hikers—few challenging rock climbs, little easy drama, just tough wild country. The best, Gary, & I've seen it all but Montana & Wyoming. This is the very best! Map in next letter, now: make triangle Yreka, Redding, Eureka. Area inside is Klamath, Salmon River, Trinity Alps, Marble Mts. Peaks 8500. Exquisite high lakes. Mild winters. Hot summers. Big runs of salmon & steelhead (all now running). Black-tail deer. Black bear. Many many foxes, no rabbits! Salmon Mts. very steep jagged tree and brush covered 1000 footers. Springs everywhere (except Rat Flat) Dan kids me "found only place with bad water in the whole country." Will tell you how I see you fitting in here in whole letter—too long for now & you sound pretty busy so what's the hurry? Yr. pome beautiful, especially last part, a whole new voice for you, very direct, I make guess that's the newest part. Am I right? I'm writing like crazy, like at Reed when on thesis. Letters from England, from Kalamazoo (honest), N.Y., all urging me on. Am I worth this great trust? I will work hard. I am strong now. Strong legs & mind.

I meant to address this with your beautiful new name (inside, not on envelope), here's a new poem Chōfū:

SONG IN RAT FLAT

Richer than the richest Falconer
I hold my hawks and canyons light as time

"Just happening along," as they say

for a flutter
for a wing-fold terrifying drop

80

(a small explosion on the ground!)

　　　　　dust & feathers rodent squeek

(his dinner's dangling down!)

　　　　　　　　　　　　Lew

To Kirby Doyle, from Forks of Salmon,
10 *October*—5 *November* 1962

Dear Kirby,　(This letter used to have another 1st page, but I can't mail it because it was silly.)
　You sound like you really need to visit me here, right on the real crust of the planet. It will set things right for you, give you the strength to *go on.* ((I love that expression as Wittgenstein used and meant it when he said "doing philosophy is successful when it shows us how to go on.")) Also, I am lonesome. I have many, many, new friends here, but none are my age. It is hard for a man to go without women, but it is harder for him to go without comrades. These letters are very important to me, but it would be far greater to be able to show you what this life of mine now is.
　The weird story of me and Lawrence Meyer continues with my present set-up. I am now living in Meyer's final house—he left here, near or over 80, and went to Sacramento and died.

　　　　PLETHORA OF HOMES
　　　　PERPLEXES POET

　　　Winter home on river,
　　　Summer estate on mountain,
　　　Fish, Game, Stanley

I came from Rat Flat with that monstrous letter to discover "you can't live up there, that place belongs to Dan Wann." So I decided there was nothing to do but see this Dan Wann and put my cards on the table.
　Dan Wann turns out to be 6′ 2 and 200 pounds, 70 years old, with white beard & 357 Magnum pistol always on hip. "No," he says, "I don't own that place, nobody owns it, old boy who built it sold me all the stuff in it, but if you want a place to write I got something better for you, it cold up there, 6 foot drifts in winter." And after I had a huge venison stew with Dan, Homer, his Indian friend (the

postman), Homer's son & various other people, he shows me this snug little place right on the river & tells me to move in. I did. Have. Am now there, settled.

It, too, was built by Lawrence Meyer (out of CCC prefab sections, not beautiful) when he finally got too old for that terrible hike up to Rat Flat. Dan calls Meyer "Horse Mountain" after the mountain Rat Flat nestles beneath.

So the cycle is complete. I am continuing *exactly* along the way Lawrence Meyer made—it even looks like I'm going to end up with his rifle! A fine old 25/35 now owned by Dan Wann's son.

So now there won't be any bad hike & you can wear your hood boots since all you have to do is walk across a swinging bridge (I am still, definitely, on the other side of the river, literally and in all senses, as Arthur used to say).

Here's what you do. Get a bus ticket to Yreka. It shouldn't cost more than $8, since that was about what it was to Reno—it might be as much as $10. Write me telling me when you'll get there & I'll meet you at the bus station & drive you here. If things foul up, wire the Yreka bus station and tell them to page me. They won't, since wires *never* arrive, but we will have tried. Best is not to miss your bus.

Bring a sleeping bag. I have everything else. Plan to stay at least a week. (anytime o.k.)

I get $100 about Nov. 1st, so make it up within that first week. I will pay return bus fare if you need it, or even drive you home since I have a few things at Albert's I need—though I hate to even think of returning even for a few days.

The dogwood is lavender. Everything else is bright yellow, except the oaks which are red and the evergreens which are that. The weather is balmy. I get up to piss and don't even have to use the coffee can. I go out to my dewy porch & sprinkle the run-off of my spring.

Oh yes, Stanley is my cat. He's not quite as nice as Yellow Fang, but who is?

Dig, it's *Yreka*, not Eureka. You go up Highway 99. Don't, repeat DO NOT try to hitchhitch. Those days are gone forever. I can even wire you bus fare after the 1st. (No I can't, it's now 5th & I am shorter than I thought, since I forgot chain saw payment in my enthusiasm.) [. . .] Always your loving Grandfather,   Lew
[P.S.] Certainly, if Diane di Prima wants to print Rat Flat Voice #1 in *Floaty Bear* I am delighted.

My desire to be always perfect tempts me to want to read that letter & make true all inaccuracies, however slight. Is that possible?

But in the meantime there are all those people who *must* be informed of all this & I still think maybe it ought to be put at the Auerhahn for my intimate friends. But, it's your letter now—do with it as you wish.   Lew

Tell Diane about mussels. (Use screw driver to help get mussels off rocks, gather about 3 dozen. *Very rich*—6-8 to a person usually enough.) Best time of year right now. Choose minus tides (tide table at any bait shop). Cook simply:

(1) boil carrots and potatoes & onions & garlic in too much water till all tender. (Celery good, too.) (Very few vegetables, you want a *weak* soup.)

Very important before (2), steam mussels in sea water till they open *then* remove top shell, clean, etc. Put a little of this sea water in broth. Keep sand out.

(2) After taking top shell off mussels & rinsing in much fresh water & removing most (but not all) seaweed, sand is the problem, get all the sand out,

(3) (big roaster best pan—2½ inch broth in roaster, *steam* mussels.) Plunk mussels in broth, cover (*add sherry!!!*)—boil *no more* than 5 or 7 minutes, & scarf. YUM YUM

[A CAT NAMED STANLEY]

From Frank Dietrich's tape of Lew Welch's class at University of California Extension, 1969-1970

I had a very lovely little cat named Stanley. And the one thing that really blew his mind was when I swept out the cabin, which I did very rarely. I was just kind of sloppy. This was when I was living alone in a mountain cabin . . . and all I had was Stanley and me, you know. He could understand everything I did, but when I started to sweep that cabin he'd sit there and watch me, man, and look at that broom and look at me and look at that broom and say, god damn! And he really couldn't dig it. What's he think he is *doing*? He was trying to figure out what this thing was *for* that I had to do. And you really get zapped, you know, and you're really together with that animal. Like sometimes, like when he died—it was a very tragic thing and . . .

Well, all right, I'm into it, I might as well tell you. This cat was out of sight, man. And he did things like he went fishing with me and went hunting with me and did all kinds of things and he was my only companion and he was just a little cat that I found. He was about *that* long and real skinny. I gave him his first full meal and we really got along very well together. He always went out at night but he was always there to wake me up in the morning. He jumped on my chest and put his nose right here and *stared*. God, it was terrible, you know. All of that was, come on, man, it's now day, you know. This morning he wasn't there and I didn't worry too much about it, and I got up and cooked and I heard this pitiful cry and Stanley was sitting by the porch with his tail bitten off, his rear leg crushed completely, no bones at all, and his offside front leg also crushed like that, and a big piece of fur about that big ripped off his back leaving the underskin so there wasn't any blood or anything, you know, just ripped off like you might rip off a piece of wallpaper. Terrible shape, I don't know how he ever got home or whatever got him. My best guess is that it might have been a big gray squirrel because it wasn't a predator. If it was a bobcat or something it would have eaten it, you know. But this was something that simply wanted to mutilate him and did and gray squirrels do do that.

So I picked him up and put him on the bed and I was horrified, you know, and he started purring and looking at me, man, and it just *blew my mind*! And so I fed him a little bit and he thought it was over, this terrible thing that had happened is now *solved*, I'm home, you know. So now I've got it and what am I going to do with it, and so I went to the old man next door and talked about it and he said, "Well, you can take him to the vet in Yreka and he might pull through, but what are you going to do with a two-legged cat especially when the two legs are on the offside and he doesn't have a tail anymore (oh, he had the most beautiful tail, big long tail) and so he won't be able to run right at all? It's just going to be a bummer. And besides he won't make it anyway." Which was pretty clear, his ribs were crushed too. So I had to shoot him!

You know that's one of the things that's important about living in the real world instead of this one that we're sitting in at the present time. If you have a dearly beloved pet, or let's say you give birth to a Mongolian idiot or any one of the natural tragedies that occur to all of us, you simply phone and make an appointment and get rid of it one way or another, don't you? In the woods you have to shoot it or bury it or keep it. It sure makes a big difference. Like you really come against these things that happen in your life. Anyway I just sat there and aimed the gun at him, you know, and I decided I'm not going to shoot him while he's looking at me—he's got to turn his head, and he looked *right* at me and he knew *exactly* what a gun was because he used to hunt with me and he deliberately turned away. Pow! right through the ear, that was it . . . Jesus, it was too much, I was broken up for weeks. Oh, it was terrible!

To Donald Allen, from Forks of Salmon, 13 *November* 1962

Dear Don,   I just learned from Gary that you'd returned to S.F. and before I could write a welcome home letter, I get yours, today, with the check.

Am I right in figuring the total sales of The Book [*The New American Poetry*] at 25,000 or thereabouts? Somebody ought to do a piece about the numbers: *Howl* at 60,000, *Like I Say* in 4th? edition, etc. etc. etc. it might persuade the more timid professors and publishers to open up a little more. They might as well face the fact that nobody else is working any more—most of the last survivors died this very year. As far as I can see there is only Us, Patchen, & Nelson Algren, & Marianne Moore, and occasionally Roethke, always with all great respect due Dr. Williams, now nearly struck out.

However, such a piece should end with the startling argument of Richard (Reb) Barker, who pointed out to me that the 60,000 figure for *Howl* was a disgrace. He got out his slide rule & figured you'd only have to sell 10 copies to the undergraduates of every university in the U.S. (not to mention England & Canada, at least) and you'd quickly get over the 100,000 mark. He claims the fault is timid merchandising—the book should have been sent out on consignment, or peddled by some live one in the student body of each school. I know he is right. I was shocked to discover almost no real book for sale at the Reed Bookstore, or at S.F. State recently—and I've met hundreds of very hip kids at both schools. At Reed, there wasn't any good place in Portland, either.

We are not being bold enough. If Ginsberg can attract 3,000 in Chicago (for *Big Table* Reading), and if people like me, with so few poems, get letters from England, Kalamazoo, and get their poems pirated in Nicaragua (I was very pleased)—there is certainly a lot going on that the big press ought to be made to admit. I don't know whether he's right or not, but Kirby says Ginsberg will have his picture on *Time* cover this year or next. I also don't know whether all this is good? or not?, but am just calling it as I see it. We have hit the young so hard, they will never be the same again. Most of them who write to me are doing it all far better and cooler than we are—tho they think we are doing lovely, exciting, unimaginable things.

I for one intend to remain just out of their sight. They'll probably invent me far nobler than I invent me, far happier, far more worthy of emulation—besides, I don't want them in their leather jackets frightening *my* mother!

I am, to answer your question, making out very well here. I am warm, well fed, not harassed by money worries, gradually becoming less paranoid (that is, less *personally* para noid: I haven't forgotten for one minute that all the governments of the world are now planning my impersonal death). Everyone on this river has been warm and generous to me. They all insist they'll make a real mountain-man out of me in nothing flat. That means I eat bear meat, venison, salmon, and get very drunk quite often. In fact, I have had to be very clever lately about refusing drink. Me! But the fact is, Don, here, I honestly prefer to be sober. It is a real relief. I am gaining weight, and, I am almost positive, have grown at least one inch! I know that isn't possible at my age, but the fact is I am now taller than people who are supposed to be (and I can see they are) about 6'2". Perhaps I just stoop less.

I am writing steadily and well. By January 1st or thereabouts (after the good hard rains set in & all the wood is cut) I hope to have finished a book of poems, some old and some new, which I will rush to your attention. So far I have about 30 pages which hold together fairly well.

I also intend to write "A Place to Put the Typewriter," a long rambling prose work about my coming to the Salmon River. I thought tonight that I might subtitle it: The Journal of a Strategic Withdrawal.

How much of this I can do will depend on the weather. It is hard for me to stay inside with all this wild country around.

Kirby says Diane di Prima wants to print a letter I wrote to him as the first issue of the western *Floating Bear*. It was something like that letter I sent to Gary which you said you read—& I intended it to be posted at Auerhahn for ALL to read. It is what the opening of "A Place to Put the Typewriter" will be partly like.

Also, I am toying with the idea of applying to Reed for a summer poet-workshop type job. However, I may not want to give the time, since I hope to build a log cabin this spring and summer. More of this in later letters.

There is too much to say. Isn't that fine!

How did you like the World? You went all the way around it and didn't tell me about it. Isn't Gary a gas? Did you sneak some poems off that crazy beautiful wife of his?

I will be in S.F. shortly after Thanksgiving. In S.F. I will probably be drunk. I will look you right up & we'll get all up to date.

I was afraid you were going to stay in Japan the rest of your life.
soon   Lew

[P.S.] You wrote what looks like *Locks of Salmon*, which is very lovely, but wrong. It is *Forks* of Salmon. The Salmon River *Forks* at that town & so they call it that. Only it isn't a town any more, it is only a Post Office and a gradually rotting Oldsmobile under a tree.

To Kirby Doyle, from Forks of Salmon, 13 *November* 1962

Kirby,   Here is an excellent new plan—requiring the discard of all former ones.

I am going to visit my mother for Thanksgiving, then come to M.V. & S.F. for that weekend and maybe a few other days. I want to pick up some things at Albert's & also Momma gets lonely.

Therefore, I can drive you UP here, instead of *Back* there. Far better to have foolproof arrival into strange country. I know I would be terrified to meet me in Yreka. Did he get the letter? Will I make the right bus? Will it break down? Is it Yreka or Eureka? Why is that man across the aisle staring at me? And the like.

Because you are even nuttier than you realize, as you will see on relaxed busride home. Your nerves will hang out of you like limp spaghetti after a week or 10 days of staring at fantastic mushrooms, fall colors & mists, spawning salmon bigger than Shannon [Doyle], not to mention huge bucks with their necks all swoll with rutting juice. (I had good shots at 2 of them today! Wild hunting trip up to Rat Flat. I lost my pack again. Missed both bucks! Lost my real Australian-issue Digger hat. Disgrace! Excitement! Legs go all wobbly when looking at a buck over the sights of a rifle. Perhaps we can go hunting.)

Also I have now but $24. If we follow new plan I will have about $80, since I'll get my stipend before return trip. Further also, you'll have longer to find sleeping bag or I can get blankets etc. which will do fine since we'll be snug inside our little cabin with wood stove going. Sleeping bag just easier and everything—also would make possible overnite stay up the hill at Rat Flat. [. . .]

Lenore writes she's deeply in love with somebody, happily settled. I am very glad for her, but find myself saying "aw shit . . ." without realizing it, it just bubbles out especially early in the morning.

Good as everything is here, much of the time I am only sad.   Lew [P.S.] Did I ever say how delighted I am that we'll be reading together? We will plan huge outrageous twin-genius love shout. Bang. Bang.

                                                        Dec. 1st, 1962
                                                        Larkspur

Second Joint Statement:

We are conscious of those within range.

                                        [signed] Lew Welch

                                        Kirby Doyle

For First Joint Statement see letter to Doyle of 1 February 1963, below.

To Philip Whalen, from Forks of Salmon, 18 December 1962

Dear Philip,   Congratulations for your beautiful poem in *Foot*, which I have now had time to read carefully & with respect.

But please tell Duerden that I am very bugged by the presentation of my poem. There are 2 bad typos (marching, when I said merging, an error which really wipes out a section I have never been able to bring off, anyway—and I further believe that I never said "ready, cool," since I avoid some of the more tired hip phrases as if they were (as they are) infected).

Now i may have been so drunk at the time i typed the poem up, in your house, from memory, that i did write that, but i am not at all sure.

the other typo is "sack" for "pack" in the opening. There are also many very ugly spacings in the poem—one whose structure is largely a matter of spacings.

why didn't i get to see the proofs? that mag hung around for months and months getting made up. there was no deadline, ever, since such a mag never has one—is only made for the fun of it so far as i can see. it seems an ideal time for a little care to be shown.

it is all i can do to accept the fact that, though very poor, i must, to work at all, work for free. i suppose i have finally accepted that.

But does it seem unreasonable to want my work to be correctly presented?

unless more respect is shown for it, my work will soon be altogether unobtainable.   Lew

[P.S.] this typewriter will seldom type caps, hence the lack of some of them in this letter. Maybe i will come to s.f. to get it fixed about xmas. will see you then.

Richard Duerden published Welch's "Hiking Poem/High Sierra" and Whalen's "Delights of Winter at the Shore" in *Foot,* no. 1.

To Kirby Doyle from Forks of Salmon, 21 December 1962

Dear Kirby,   I never properly acknowledged your beautiful letter in answer to my Rat Flat Voice, wherein you said so much better than I generally do the vision we all have of this generous, easy planet—& all us fighting on top of it—especially lately.

And I worry that maybe when you were here you were disappointed, not by the planet but by me—the way I move on it, even here.

I'm afraid I am still not making it—tho all I say about this country is true, & all I say about me in it, making it, is true.

Many days I survive only by making the joke that this is a rest home & I am not permitted out of bed anyway (so I can stay in the sack & not even take my needed shit "until 10:30"). At 10:30 I do that, pretending I must do it then or never. The rest of the day proceeds with various therapies—which I cleverly have arranged to be timed in such a way I may *or may not* accept.

The phantom nurses and doctors are very lenient.

It all works, finally, because of the total lack of fear here (which I know you felt). Finally I can go whole days in loose joy, looking at things, helping others, writing, working prodigiously at real things like "getting in the wood" or, as they say in these parts, "making wood."

Today, for example, I began to cut down trees to "make my wood" & my great chain saw fucked up & so I went to Homer's to see if he could fix it. On the way to his place I had to stop at Sally Novak's (since she was walking the baby in the road & to ignore her would be a genuine, direct rebuff). In the next half hour of trying to find the right tool in her husband's tool box I learned that there is a trained nurse at the Forks of Salmon where we should have taken you to stitch up your hand. We are a "depressed" area & can get *all* attention free. Sorry, Kirby, I didn't know.

It turns out that this is a Magic Mountain, written by Kafka, & I have been, as usual, slow to pick up.

It is also (and *only*, really) the undisguised Planet Earth (if one could only see it).

And then I finally got to Homer's & he fixed my chain saw & I played darts with his son David & we had to milk the cow. The whole family went away & they gave me all the day's milk.

On the way home I wrote the best poem I've written here yet:

A CHRISTMAS CARD TO THE BENNETTS, IN THE FORM OF A THANK YOU NOTE.

Dear Homer, Doris, David, Kathy, and Homer Jr.
I came to your house with a busted saw and the worry I'd be
    cold all winter.
I left your house with tools for my saw & a gallon of milk.

Driving home, I felt: "What more could a man possibly want?"
Thank you,
                    Lew Welch

They say that Bo-Jew-E (I transliterate, not remembering the accepted French form) used to take his poems down the road & show them to an illiterate farm lady. If she didn't dig them, he changed them, & still retained all his subtle references to the "old poems"etc.

It is possible to reach people who don't read, without writing "down" to them. If you do this just right you reach everybody else, too. This is the cross-eyed bear. I often wish I didn't—how I envy Duncan his "room."

Laughter came down the mountain singing badly out of tune.

90

That's how I want to write—not even for me!

* * * *

I worry that you didn't enjoy your stay here for lack of the real mountain guide I am when not mortally ill. As for me, I enjoyed your visit enormously & look forward to another when the Drs. allow—about April & afterwards, so I understand.

Perhaps by then I will be out. Let us hope so.

Huge productions! New works! (then my typewriter broke.) Maybe I come fix him about Xmas & see you.

Meanwhile, best to your beautiful Dee & Shannon & you   Lew

Bo-Jew-E: probably Po Chu-I.

1963

To Philip Whalen, from Forks of Salmon, 2 January 1963

Dear Phil — Please pretend I never wrote my last letter. I am not at all displeased, tho I must have been for about the 10 minutes it took to write that gibberish. "Cabin fever," in these parts, is called "getting shack-simple." I hope you didn't let Duerden know of my disordered condition, but if you did, please offer my deepest apologies. Otherwise, all is well here. The cramp in my head is almost gone—there is only an occasional spasm   Lew

To Philip Whalen, from Forks of Salmon,
"Sometime in January 1963"

Dear Phil,   I didn't come to S.F. for Christmas because it was so soon after my Thanksgiving trip & had just gotten back into the drift of things here—in fact, found myself into a new phase: "The Settling In" as they'd say in *I Ching.*

The therapy part of this venture seems to have worked at last. I putter around cleaning things and arranging things, up all night, then asleep for days, all troubles dissolved out of my head. Read Balzac's *Séraphîta*—a nice Swedenborgian/Christian candy bar all about how an angel is all light and no sex and can talk about anything—like they *KNOW*, man! But it's all worked up in a big ice landscape that is very high and fine. Then read *The Alkahest,* which is easily the most beautiful novel of family love ever imagined & have thus learned that Balzac is a dandy. I imagine you and/or Albert must have some of his works. I intend to read the whole Comedy if it's all been translated (somehow never, until now, read Balzac except painfully in College French ((a terrible passage all about banisters and other architectural nouns))).

This letter by hand because my typewriter broke TWICE & it's 300 miles back and forth (75 miles each way taking & leaving &

picking it up) and all my money spent on it & then it breaks again, which literally sends me to bed all day *smashed* my whole life ruined, the whole Universe trying to keep me from writing, I can't THINK with a pen!

So new peace of mind easily DESTROYED

But it's starting to uncramp—whole days of easy bliss, things seen, understood, it's all all right.

(And then my chain saw broke. And then my Coleman. It's an epidemic of "thing trouble") ((There are no inanimate objects))

(not one!   )

So I'm still not "right," not where I want to be, have been, am now and then.

I scribble a little with this pen (it's been a month now) so if it ever happens that I have a typewriter again I might have something written down by spring.

I have no idea why anybody (and there seems to be several) should want me to say ALL & give me all that encouragement and everything. But it makes me feel better to hear them say it & I will try not to be a big disappointment. Also I get sick if I don't write more or less as the main thing I do all day, but lately it has only been the same old tirade out of a mind that is only bitter & can only hate. There is plenty of such stuff around (viz. last issue of *Evergreen*) and it just ought not to see the light of day.

Also I am lazy. I have been thinking about why I am lazy. There are lots of reasons. Maybe if I stay up here where it's pretty and quiet, and maybe if I take long walks and never read the news-papers (even the old ones (('60, 61)) I start fires with), maybe all the reasons, and lack of reasons, will go away. I hope so.

I haven't had a letter from my mother in almost a month & really am worried. I fear she failed that Civil Service exam for the 3rd time which means she'll lose her job & feel sure I'll hate her because she can't give me my therapy money as long as promised. Of course I won't hate her at all—knew, months ago, she'd fail the exam (it isn't in her field & she can't study, can't read even, on her own)—and knew the help would not last the promised year—in fact, have been amazed it lasted this long & took it in the first place only because I had nowhere else to go but out.

I think I am now in good enough shape to go dollar grubbing again, here, on this river, where all kinds of jobs open up in the spring & where I have, at least, a rent free place to live where I

don't bother anyone. Also I can survive here for $40 worth of groceries each month & have less reason to drink (or to want to drink
((dollars or no))). It doesn't seem quite so hopeless here. I can try
for a base $480.00 and know that once that's in I'll be warm and fed
for a year (tho I'll need some extra for the inevitable broken typewriter & aching tooth).

I apologize for bringing up this subject, as unpleasant to you as it
is to me.

(I STOP)

Maybe I'll drop by in February to see you all. I feel like it.

Tell Jack [Kerouac] of course I ain't mad at him. Why should I
be? Also I would write him if I knew where he was, is.

I thot this was gone be a cheerful letter. too bad.

Mostly I'm O.K. Best in years. How are you? Tell everybody I'm
up here in my mountain cabin and I have long undies on, but it's
much warmer than Japan.

Gary wrote a nice rambly Rohatsu letter. I think he's got the
right way.

I don't really like birds
They're practically reptiles

love, Lew

To Kirby Doyle, from Forks of Salmon, 1 February 1963

Dear Kirby,   the more I think about it, the more I am convinced
that the world *needs* our one-issue *Joint Statement.* Here is what I
propose.
  1. Let's begin collecting the material. It won't cost us anything
     & will be a gas.
  2. When we have nearly enough stuff (or right now, for that
     matter), let's run an ad in *Evergreen* asking for $2,000 & explaining that as much money will be paid contributors as will
     be paid to union journeymen & ink & paper companies. Even
     if we fail to get the dough such an ad will make its revolutionary mark.
Wally [Berman] should be art director & we all go down to L.A. for
the make-up.

The *Notes about Contributors* section should include:
LEO KEELER chewed gum constantly between the ages of 12
and 18 because he believed masturbators could be detected
by their breath.

I am planning a long list of things to do. The piece is called
"Free Trips, Available to All." Here's one:
The next time there is a warm, light rain go to the park and lie
down on your back in some nice grassy spot. Look directly up
into the rain. Try not to blink when a raindrop is coming
directly at your eye.
This list will be signed Jimmy Vahey.

Nearly everything should be contributed by you and me, under
various fake names, but *all of them traceable.* This way we not
only insure that the magazine will contain really first-rate stuff, but
also we can assure ourselves most of the loot.

Here is another great "Free Trip":
Submerge your head in the toilet bowl.
Open your eyes
Another:
Go downtown and look at everybody. Look only at their ears.
Think about ears. Try to see a person as being 2 ears with a
nearly round divider in between. Practice this until you *only*
are aware of ears. Now look into a mirror.
One of your (traceable) names could be: Helmet Head.

· · · · · · · · · ·

I am in the middle of an exquisite natural high. It was brought
about by boredom & loneliness. Anything faced, directly, will
vanish. I have vanished.
This is my original face before my mother and father were born.

· · · · · · · · · ·

Maybe I will come see you the first week of February. Won't
that be fun?

· · · · · · · · · ·

The other morning I got this one:

I don't really like birds
They're practically reptiles

I attach a poem. I send my love to you and your beautiful girl.   Lew

I saw myself
a ring of bone
in the clear stream
of all of it

and vowed
always to be open to it
that all of it
might flow through

and then heard
"ring of bone" where
ring is what a
bell does

To Gary Snyder, from Forks of Salmon, 1 *February* 1963

Dear Chōfū   Me & my CCC Cabin (both of us obsolete, I for
practicing my ancient art, and he because he's just sitting here
without the reason for his being here or anywhere anymore) are
now enjoying the first rain of spring. Phil writes that you and J. Eliz.
were freeeeezing all winter. Too bad. Here, it never got below 8°
& was up to 40 or 50 every day. Not one bit of snow down here in
the river channel, tho a small amount fell on the ranges over 6,000
(I am only at 1,500). But no sun ever hits this cabin in winter & frost
was all over everything since Thanksgiving. I never saw frost so
pretty. Bright white frost flowers as long as your finger growing out
of all rocks, stumps, etc. I meant to take photos but now the warm
rain has washed it all away & I'll have to wait till next year &
maybe I'll be far away by then.

   When it rains here the landscape goes into a Sung painting. For-
ested peaks (without bases) floating in a gray sky. The river rises
alarmingly fast because of the steep watershed—it is 5 feet higher
today after only one day and one night of heavy rain. I have to
keep a small fire in the cookstove or it gets chilly, but with any fire
big enough to keep going gets the place (10 feet × 20 with a ceiling
only a half inch over 6 feet) too hot, so I open both doors and stay
warm radiantly & have sweet cool spring-rain air to breathe. The
disappearance of the frost reveals moss-green grass.

   I didn't get here, settled, soon enough to get enough wood in so
have been burning green madrone. I just cut the madrones down

to get them out of the way of a smallish dead fir, never dreaming I could use the madrone itself until maybe summer. But then I ran out of wood and tried it & it is just dandy. It burns with a fuchsia & lime-green flame like funny combined color on saris. Very hot and long lasting when you finally coax it to burn. Also I sliced up a fallen oak about 8 inches in diameter & it burns with a wonderful peppery smell as strong as, tho entirely different from, sandalwood. I also have bark both wet and dry (and also sound or rotten) so I mix up wood stews for various heating effects & to amuse myself.

I honestly believe that way over half the troubles in the world would vanish if everyone had a wood stove and fuel to burn in it.

I stupidly goofed on the fuel mixture for my fine McCulloch saw and burned it up bad. I need at least a new rod, maybe a new piston & rebored cylinder. It stopped the same day my typewriter broke & that night one of my Coleman lanterns quit. There are no inanimate objects. I got so upset I spent the whole of the next day in bed thinking up fantasies about 2 young girls and a knobby gourd.

I can see by the way this letter is going that I'm "shack-simple" again. (A fine expression I learned on this river.) I often get very bored & lonely here, but have discovered the hermit delights of sweeping, cleaning, oiling, fixing, rearranging, building shelves & other carpentry work, and daily target practice with assorted arms. Also I met a fine fellow, a painter named Jack Boyce. He is intelligent, hip & disgusted with everything and a great lush. Also he can afford to buy good booze. So every week or so I drive 20 miles to his place, or he drives 20 to mine, and we get plastered and talk all night long, fix breakfast, and then part (I sleep all that next day). We usually polish off 2 fifths of whiskey & recently solved all world, art, moral, political, & religious problems except one: how to get Jack to paint. Jack is one of those artists who spends all his time trying not to be a painter, and who fails nevertheless. He is stuck with it & only needs a small nudge from or into the right direction & he'll blow like crazy. I intend to take him to S.F. in February to see if a tour of our beautiful friends will help. The poor bastard has seen only the dirty, shiftless, hate-filled, doped up unhiply, lack-genius side of this whole generation. It is not really his fault either. Sometime I will tell how ugly it's getting, man.

On the [last] page is a list of equipment I've acquired since I got here. It just goes to show you what you can do with a steady $100 a month if you don't have to pay rent or buy fuel and water, and if you take it easy on the booze. Everything there, except the rifle (a sweet 30-30 Marlin w/strap & peep sight), I bought myself. The rifle was a Christmas present.

Now here is what I wanted to talk to you about: If you, as you usually do, keep grinding away at your present studies, it is possible that you may arrive here all enlightened with a black belt or perhaps even a bowl & mantle—at any rate with a Roshi diploma & with a desire to set up a Zendo of some kind or other. If you want me to, I could have a wide choice of spots on this river for you to choose from. I already have one valid claim of 20 acres & have the first call on Rat Flat & this spring will claim 3 or 4 places I've spotted up a beautiful creek. Curious & ugly doings in Washington are trying to make all gold claims invalid, laws are changing, new things coming up all the time (for example, you can now *buy* 5 acres ((only)) without timber water or mineral rights, for $125. I plan to look into this deal for myself, since I don't want to fake gold-mining if it will mean ugly official pestering. Also there is a "special use" permit on 99-year lease that ought to be a cinch for a bona fide religious organization. Then there is always the claim law, though that is now under heavy fire as I say).

Anyhow, if you want me to I can be your advance scout & have things all under control when you finally need it, if at all.

I don't think there is a better location in America. It is beautiful, with mild weather, wild, cheap, and only 8 hours from S.F. by good roads. There really is good gold here, too. A Zendo of even 20 monks working only 4 or so hours a day could pay all expenses with ease. The only problem here is labor, that is the *only* reason no one is mining.

What I thought might be a gas is to have a setup that ran only for the 2 big sesshins, with maybe an advance group to set the place straight for the monks. All buildings log or shake cabins. (I will have built mine by then and could be foreman & designer—there are many tricky things about building with logs & designing correctly for them.)

Or maybe you and J. Eliz. might want a little spread just for yourselves, in which case I'd sign over one of mine to you guys. Rat Flat, it turns out, will be right in the middle of a huge logging operation & may be surrounded by dismal desolation. But it is yours if I can hold it & if you should want it.

This spring & summer I'll work for the Forestry & will get everything about laws etc. absolutely straight. I have decided not to start building on my claim till I know exactly what's going on (also, I need a little bread for windows, flooring, stove, heater, water pipe, etc. etc.).

But it looks like I'll hang around here at least till next winter, maybe the rest of my life. I have permission to stay in this little CCC shack as long as the present owner lives. There are also other places. I'm set up real good.

I no longer am wildly excited by this country, it just suits me. I get bored and lonely, but then I think of the alternative living patterns & realize this is just right for me. I can always split for a month or two if I want, there is work here in summer, it's pretty, cheap, and very easy all around. I don't see any point in bucking hard weather, either. This country is astonishing in that way.

Write and tell me what you think about all this.

I do zazen in a crazy little grotto I found about 20 minutes walk from here. I sit on a mossy boulder staring at a little brook about 3 feet wide and swift. Lovely music. Across my lap is my rifle. Deer come by and I don't shoot them. Soon I will shoot one just to see how that goes—also I get hungry 'long about the end of the month: have to eat mush all day. A poem came while sitting there. It begins:

> I burn up the deer in my body
> I burn up the trees in my stove

If you do set up a Zendo I won't join. I eat meat & sit better all alone and wild. I hate all organizations. I will only help set it up & maybe be gold-mining foreman. I took "original face" for my koan. Very difficult, but it is starting to dissolve. I hate that damn koan, but that is what I want to figure out. I don't give a damn about clapping or dogs.

This spring I intend to do quiet manicuring of my sitting place. If you get here I'll take you there. I walk to it, sit about one hour, walk back—altogether just under 2 hours with much walking. I have best zazen walking. I will bring that official bell we used to use at Marin-an. I need that bell. Also I will set up incense on rock. Now I have only my rifle.

I may plant a plum tree, or a wild apple. I may plant wild grapes —they are all over here.

Many new poems, some of them dandies,   blow Chōfū,   Lew [P.S.] Also, thanks for great pictures. Have them pinned on wall— you, Peter, Allen with big mountains is wild flick. I will send pictures soon.

99

Have absolutely broken old "no-home" problem. It dissolves into meaninglessness. With *that* off my mind, all cramps in head now loosening. Old man 'cross river started me on right track. His place his "camp" tho lived there 30 years.

List of Equipment acquired between October & February

Chain saw w/30″ bar
2 Axes (Kelly & Collins Dble. Bit, found in woods)
2 Coleman Lanterns (one single, one double) (dble., a gift)
1 Kerosene Cabin Lantern
5 gal. Propane tank (full)*
Propane 2 burner gas plate*
Steel Cot (gift from old Bill Allen)
Boots (Chippewa w/Italian soles)
Rifle (gift. 2nd hand at Abercrombie Fitch, good deal)
Dutch Oven (lid is also cast iron fry pan)
Double boiler
2 gal. Forestry approved gas can for chain saw
Dishpan
Dishes, cups, bowls, etc.
Hammer
Chain saw wrenches & screwdrivers
Scissors
$20 Typewriter repair & cleaning
Ream of typing paper
2 6-ply tires
20 acre Mining Claim
Use of 2 excellent Cabins, free.

To Buy this Summer

Sleeping bag (4-lb. Dacron just right here)
Kelty Pack
Light Moc-toe Summer Boots (Wolverine, if sole right)

Deerskin hunting shirt (as birthday gift?)
2½× Scope for Marlin Rifle (if gold or fire-money bonanza)

*Didn't really need these, but planned to put them in Rat Flat for cooking. Heavy, but 3 months cooking for $1.75 fuel & very handy, safe, etc. May sell it, or maybe use it for summer cooking if cook-stove too hot. Got whole outfit real cheap from old Bill Allen.

Rock-hound hammer   (By the way, yr. Geology idea a great
                    one. I want to study that too. May start
                    huge library project—I get books in
                    Yreka for one month.

To Jack Kerouac, from Forks of Salmon, 7 March 1963

Dear Jack,   Whalen tells me you're worried that I'm worried or
mad or something. There is nothing you could ever do that would
bug me, except maybe momentarily. And if you're afraid I might
be bugged by how I came out in *Big Sur*, I can't see anything but
praises for a guy who drives well, can use an axe, fry fish, and who
is sometimes a tiresome explainer. Say whatever you like about
Lew Welch. I am tired of him. I spend most my time trying to rid
my original face of Lew Welch, but he keeps hanging around inside me and fucking everything up. He is no friend of mine, even
though I think he is very gifted and handsome.
   I miss your big red face. How are you? What are you doing back
in Northport?
   I thought *Big Sur* was a damned fine book & told everybody so. I
also know that you felt even worse than that, as Lenore & I knew
at the time, as you said in the book.
   There is something haunted about Big Sur. I went back to that
same cabin (after leaving Lenore, both of us in tears) and cracked
up or cracked out, more painfully than I have ever— and I crack
often: it's the only way I know to grow, like a crab splitting out of
his shell and sitting around naked waiting for the new, bigger one
to grow. It would be better if I never grew another one, but I
always do, and the damned thing always looks and acts exactly like
Lew Welch.
   When what I really am is a Lion in the shape of a man, with a
belly full of bees and honey, as we all know.
   Big Sur is very fierce and haunted and spooky. However, it is
important to go there and crack up. If you really crack up in Big
Sur, you understand all about Druids and old dark Oracles. I think
there ought to be a Zendo in Big Sur, with a Roshi who wears a
long white beard, like Death, and who beats you with a gnarled
oak limb. He should speak only in tongues and wear seaweed and
redwood bark. Maybe I will be that Roshi, as I said in a poem I
wrote . . .

Let all my wildness free until
Those about their fires at twilight or at dawn
Shall say "That?
Oh that is just that thin red man howling again
Howling
in his hills of

SUR!"

But right now I live in a town with the improbable name of Forks
of Salmon where the ghost of a gentle old Wobbly keeps watch
over me, finds me cabins, friends, and points out game (he likes to
go hunting).

I wear good mountain boots, carry a rifle always, and live in a
CCC cabin. I am on the other side of the river. There is a crazy
swinging bridge of rotten boards and rusty cables. A coon takes his
shit almost every day on the bridge, right at its start on the other
side. I don't know whether he does it out of malevolence or fear or
what (animals seldom cross these bridges—that is how we know
they don't have Buddha nature: they never get to the other side of
the river).

Now it is spring. There was a butterfly (orange) on the coon turd
yesterday.

For the first time in my life I don't have money worries. I was so
bad this last time that Mom said either it's the nut house or Japan
or the woods. I chose the woods & she sends me $100 a month. So
I can at last buy food and booze and flashlights and new boots and
don't have to always worry. But it will end about May & then I'll
try working for the Forestry. I don't know whether I can or not,
I'm really too crazy to work anymore, but everybody on this river
is crazy so maybe they won't notice. How will I ever get up?

Maybe I'll win a Nobel Prize or something and won't have to.

I now write very well indeed. I'm putting all my poems together
into a book called "EarthBook" (so spelled) and will make somebody publish it with a photo of a beautiful mossy rock on the
cover. It's the rock I do zazen under, it's almost a little cave. A
brook with lots of waterfalls flows right below it. Deer walk by and
I don't shoot them.

If everything keeps going as it is right now I will soon be a
Buddha and will save you all. So don't worry.

I attach a poem. Many many poems like that.   and send my
love,   Lew

PS Kirby Doyle and I read April 5, 6, 7 in San Francisco, Big Sur and Monterey—a bash! You will hear reverberations in Northport. Or fly out and hear us—we could exorcise all evil from Bixby Canyon, scratch Alf, and take a mineral bath.
This is the first of a group of 12 small lyrics called "Songs in Rat Flat."

[Enc. "Farewell to His Birds and Animals"]

To Philip Whalen, from Forks of Salmon, 15 March 1963

Dear Philip—All that good news! Everybody *werkin'* (as the old Swede on the fishboat said). Me, too. All my poems are nearly collected in "EarthBook" for market. I wrote Jack a long letter. Many new poems, all mantic. It snowed for 1st time *all year!* yesterday. Sunny today. I will arrive 3/26 or so to get *up* for reading etc love, Lew

To Gary Snyder, from Forks of Salmon, 22 March 1963

Dear Gary,   They are blasting the road across from where I live and today I got 9 perfect, brand-new, powder boxes! The very best ones—with the dovetailed corners and the thick wood! Tomorrow I think I can get 6 more!
I had to tell you this good news at once, especially since you are the only person in the world who is as much of a box freak as I am. I think I will put shelves in one of them, like I did at Reed—do you still have that box?
I wrote you and J. Eliz. a long long letter months ago, but am never in a Post Office, or if I am I forget to buy the stamps, or if I remember I don't have 50¢. I am going to S.F. for a giant reading there & in Big Sur & Monterey & I promise to mail the letter, then.
I am writing so many poems I'm beginning to wonder if maybe my critical faculties have left me. Everything I say seems to be absolutely true and beautiful. Also the meters are lovely. All my poems going into a big book called "EarthBook" which I will lay on Don Allen next week with orders to get it published.
Phil says J. Eliz. has cut off all her hair, never drinks anymore, and is writing beautiful poems. As I understand it, it has something

103

to do with finally beginning *just barely* to see what flower arranging is about. Ask her to please write me. The reports are very conflicting. Nemi [Frost] has a lot of letters from her that don't say anything like that at all. We all have decided you have about 7 wives, each with the duty of writing to one of us. The one who is supposed to write to me never does & it makes me sad.

Is it true that you may be coming to U.S. next fall? I hope so. I don't know where I'll be by then, but prolly I'll be limping back here. Right now I'm swinging so hard I feel lonely and bored in these woods. I think everything is going to break wide open this year—all good. Everyone in S.F. working, happy, with a little bread even (except poor Philip). It is another & different pulse. Everyone tired of putting the Beat Generation in jail, now I think they'll sit back and listen and laugh. Ginsberg on the cover of *Time*, etc.

I plan a huge book to be called "Bread"—a frank challenge to this economy. Why can't we afford poetry? Lamantia, Kirby, Meltzer & I vowed to have mss. in my hands July 1st. I wrote Duncan about it, will tell Phil & McClure. That ought to be enough. I don't want it to be an angry, bitter book—I want it to *end* the fake (PW: "immoral") war between the hip and the square. I want it to make a frank appeal for *patronage* & to be directed squarely at people with real money, none of whom, I feel, realize how little it takes to keep a poet alive: that $1500 a year to a man like Whalen will change the world forever. And I want it to make the point that what is needed is rent money, food money, bread! The rest takes care of itself. We want to give the *poetry* away. Etc. Definitely want something from you, if you're interested. This could be very big, Gary. Huge plans. Will write in more detail, later. In short, I see this as the right moment to challenge & change a totally unexamined cultural attitude, a dangerous attitude that is hurting everyone. How can you write true poetry if you're forced by poverty to sing through rotten teeth? I don't really think anyone wants us to. They just haven't thought about it. When challenged all but the real rotten bastards are on my side in about ½ an hour. And part of it is our fault. Those French Impressionists stood flatly against, outside, etc., and made a stance unheard of in history. And many of us assume that stance without seeing how foolish it is. It does nobody any good. Ginsberg's simple stance of: I am a Poet, Poets try to be great men, men of love, *that* is more like it.

I understand all the complicated reasons for a natural antipathy toward anything creative, but I say let's forget those *reasons* and charm the poor babies out of their lives. Etc. I read my poems to people on this river and they stop their cheap bullshit and act as if being a poet is not so foolish after all. Or put it this way: We have taken Poetry out of the libraries, but we still haven't gotten it into the homes of people who need to read it. It is partly our fault.

Well anyhow I have solved the box problem, perfectly, for the rest of my life. Now I'm going to be Lawrence of America on Racing Camel Corvette (or Scarab?) with saddlebags of gold for poetry, for Bread!   love,   Lew

To Donald Allen, from Forks of Salmon, 18 *April* 1963

Dear Don,   I think it is important to include the attached with my "Songs in Rat Flat." Otherwise the title will be only a meaningless Connorism—out of place.

●

I got back here to find a blizzard going on. Very corny Japanese effect of snow on branches of salmon-colored peach blossoms.

Now it is raining, warm, river swollen and steelhead jumping over falls.

I haven't forgotten that I cracked your Zen bell. I've asked Gary to forward you another.

●

One more month and my dole ends, so will try for work with the Forestry. It's a good deadline for getting the book to Scribner's. As we agreed, I'll send you a copy of the book.

Thanks very much for suggesting Scribner's, giving me the names, and offering a letter.

I wrassle with carbons.   Lew
[Enc.] Note to be printed at the end of "Songs in Rat Flat"
"Rat Flat is the name I gave to a beautiful cabin I found this winter in the mountains of northern California. An old Wobbly named Lawrence Meyer built the cabin entirely out of material from the woods: Shakes (big shingles) hand-split from sugar pine, natural poles for braces, doors of hewn oak. The interior weathered a uniform golden color, and on a sunny day, or when I lit my kerosene lamp, it was like living in a Vermeer.

These poems are further dedicated to Lawrence Meyer, then, whose ghost led me eerily to his place at a time of great need, and who knew what it meant: "shaped as wood can be when a man has had his hand to it."

To Lew Welch, from Marianne Moore, 260 Cumberland Street, Brooklyn, 27 April 1963

Very exact, Mr. Welch—WOBBLY ROCK. My thanks.
     Did not see your letter, just the Rock at first.
     You really can write—one reason I let Mrs. V D persuade me to review the Anthology   Marianne Moore

Irita Van Doren, then editor of the *New York Herald Tribune Book Review*, asked Marianne Moore to review *The New American Poetry* in June 1960.

To Kirby Doyle, from Forks of Salmon, 1 May 1963

Dear Kirby,   Where are you?
     The silence is killing me, so am now going around with a gold-pan. No gold, yet.
     I don't know what I'm doing, but the weather is beautiful.   Lew

To Philip Whalen, from Forks of Salmon, 3 May 1963

Dear Philip,   The whirly-bird landed me in a blizzard somewhere between the forks of this river, high above my cabin. The next day was sunny. Peach blooms covered with snow and other corny effects of abortive spring.
     I am reading Rilke & I think that Mr. Rilke is right. I don't remember Robert Duncan ever mentioning a debt to R., but it sure sounds like Robert. Also he has a world of Things which exist quite strangely, as Robert's Things do, but it all turns out that Things are happy, even though they FALL. Mr. MacIntyre is often irritated by Rilke. What I like about the Elegies is the form of many connected long poems, but not too long, which exist in series (unlike, say, Pound's *Cantos* & Chas. O's [Maximus] Letters) so that "deeper meanings . . . darker thoughts" can gather as you go along. Also I

like the serene tone of Rilke, especially because he can't really hold it down forever & you get a little explosion at the end, or here and there in the middle.

All of this is helping me to clarify the many problems of "Spring Rain Revolution at the Forks," which I am presently cranking up into shape. Despite ovations and all, the poem simply isn't there yet. It is so much in my Mind, however, that I think what Meltzer, say, *heard* is absolutely accurate. I fear that all you have to do is have something strongly on your mind and the *sound* comes through whatever is written down (when, that is, you read it out loud). In Big Sur, for example, about 6 of us listened to an 18 month old person explain his toys with breathtaking accuracy and fluency in a language of squeeks and goos and gestures. A tape-recording of his "reading," however, would reveal that "nothing was said."

I brought a lot of *New Yorkers* here from my mother's heap in the living room, and discovered that Dwight MacDonald recently learned to his horror that 35,000,000 Americans are living in poverty (about 23%!!!!, he says). Another source (*Post*) said that the Ford Foundation spends $700,000,000 per annum for "welfare" (people like your friend Untermeyer) and that it (the Ford Foundation) is the "genius and flower of the American free enterprise system." Still another source (the *S.F. Chronicle*) reports that Mr. (or Mrs.) Kennedy's sister, who has a "mentally retarded" child, discovered that only $33,000,000 per annum is spent on pre & post natal care for needy mothers, but that 98,000,000 dollars are spent on the birth care of *pedigreed cows*! She is incensed! — As mustn't we all very well *be*!

These figures to cheer you up in the midst of your present difficulties.

Gary writes that he has no desire whatever to be a Roshi & that even if he were a Roshi he would not limit my diet to vegetables. He also said that he and Joanne will visit us in January. He also said that "we, or I" might be interested in a cabin up here (I had offered to look around for a claim for him). What does the "or I" mean?

I got my last $100 dole check & have already (last month) spent $50 of it (because of the disappointing financial aspects of the reading tour: I made $30). I intend to go to Medford Monday and buy $50 worth of dried beans (which I despise) so that I can survive yet a little while longer. The Forestry has laid off (layed off?) (shoved it to?) all its crews because they claim not to have any budget already. Maybe a new budget comes up in June (fire season). "all its crews" means the seasonal gangs, of course. The others are still waxing fat.

Meanwhile, I have a gold-pan and a sluice-box and intend to "snipe" for gold. It will keep me off the streets and perhaps even out of the doldrums of despair. I am not strong. I see the growth of panic already.

It's too bad Doubleday doesn't want your book. Have you thought of Scribners? Have you thought of the Saxon grant? Have you thought of Howard Hughes? Have you thought of becoming a pedigreed cow, or of faking muscular dystrophy?

Why don't you go to Europe?, that's what you should do. Why don't you get married and settle down, buy a place of your own and get to work?

It is very nice of Tommy [Sales] to put you up. Don Allen said you wanted to get back to the city. Please say hello to Tommy and assure her that though I seem to act as if she doesn't exist (we haven't met for years, I suddenly realize), I think of her often. Rachel must be large and beautiful.

I must stop this and wire my Broker at once. The bastard acts as if there weren't such a thing as taxes at all. I told him to lose that $90,000 but he used it to back the Seattle Fair and I made 8%. What the fuck is the world coming to!   Lew

"Mr. MacIntyre": C. F. MacIntyre, a translator of Rilke.

To Dorothy Brownfield, from Forks of Salmon, 8 May 1963

Dear Mom,   Happy Birthday and Mother's Day. I attach a silly poem.

We just went to Medford to buy groceries. A nice town.

How is Tramp? What news?   Love,   Lew

Invitation to the Kirby Doyle-Lew Welch reading at Batman Gallery,
13 May 1961.

The *Chico* and Lew Welch.

The Forks of Salmon cabin.

The bridge at Forks of Salmon and Jack Boyce with Lew Welch in the bar at Cecilville.

BIRTHDAY POEM, WITH INSTRUCTIONS, TO HIS MOTHER

Now that you are sixty-one
Time's ripe for you to have some fun with
Welfare State.

Begin this hard-won new enjoyment
By descending on state Unemployment
In tiny flowered hat and tennis shoes.

Tell them you are old and sick.
Make of age a fearsome stick to beat down
Dollars from the Tax Tree!

Throw a tantrum, wet your pants, be
Terrible as all our Widowed Aunts have been for
Centuries.

When the office opens shop
Be there with bucket and with mop
Beseeching them for work!

Pretend you cannot fill out forms
(Your eyes are weak. The worms of age have
Eaten at your memory.)

This way, Clerks will fill them out
And make your case beyond a doubt the
Tightest in their files.

And when the Money does come in,
Always snarl, never grin:
"It surely isn't *very much*, young man!"

Then down to Abercrombie Fitch
For sleeping bags and rich wool
Scarves and other things.

Go camping in the Wild West.
In Virgin Rivers swim, and rest
Beneath the sighing pine boughs.

Northward on to clean Seattle,
Where finally you drop this agéd prattle
And look for work befitting to your dignity . . .

In short, begin to use your age to bilk the dirty rats!
Enjoy yourself. And when you're done

Leave half a million dollars to your cats.

*To Lew Welch, from Marianne Moore, 260 Cumberland Street,
Brooklyn, 11 May 1963*

Thank you, Mr. Welch, for parting with one of your *Wobbly Rock*s
and noticing that I *noticed* some things in your work—that I notice
the "hand-crafted" quality.

Robert Graves when he read at Hunter College on the 9th, said, I
think he said (quoting Goethe), "Genius is not superhuman exertion
but naturalness."

This needs no answer. You haven't time.   Marianne Moore

To Gary Snyder, from Forks of Salmon, 14 May 1963

Dear Gary,   I suppose I got onto those romantic notions re: Zendos
& all because of too much time alone. Shack simple. Yes, it is already different. / I got bit by a scorpeen, not even as bad as à bee.
Then I rooted out poison oak and came on all puffy. No itch, just a
swollen face & balls very red and burning like a sunburn & a fever.
Lovely dreams. Puking. No blisters & today it's almost gone away. I
had a meditation & talked to my body telling it to stop the silly allergic bullshit. / Today I went gold mining for first time. Panned up
some big pyrite ("Pirates" on this river) crystals but no gold. Then I
took my rifle out because I didn't really know whether it shot real
straight. Found it groups under 3″ at 100 yards, excellent for a
30-30 (one group less than an inch for 3 shots). But all very high (as
I suspected). After all testing was over I said, all right, let's put one
in the bull's-eye and go home. Whop, dead center. I intend to be
the first Zen rifleman. Will show anyone who wishes how to shoot
himself thru the barrel. You learn where the bullet is going to end
up and then you pin the target on it. / It's finally Spring! I and all
the other creatures and green things are very glad. I been cooped
up thinking too much. I quit for a while. Cut all my hair off mountain style & don't have a poem in me. Good. Tomorrow I go to the
Forestry to try to get a trail crew job. I want to learn to handle

stock, throw Vajra etc. Also I want to see all of this country. But the word is that no one will be hired till July because of no budget and wet spring. In that case I'll go gold hunting in a serious & systematic way. I have 2 good spots lined up ("unfinished business" of a pair of miners who don't care anymore & put me on to them). Maybe I'll make a couple bucks. Very hypnotising work. The next shovel-full might just be! But 4 hours without a "color" proved to be the limit of my patience. Also, the creeks are very pretty. A mink came down to drink. Sandwiches dunked in cold water, etc. / I get very bugged with myself, this cabin, these mountains & this river. But then I can't think where else I'd rather be, even if I could afford it. Maybe I'm hooked. I hope to be able to save enough this summer to winter in S.F. at least for a month or 2. However, tomorrow I'm going to fall a big tree with my McCulloch & slice it up so it'll be dry, in case I have to hole up here again. / Please send plans for Jap bathtub as per one of yr. letters. I'm very curious. Very good news that you're coming over in January. All the car pets will be spread. What is the best translation of the *Diamond Sutra*? I lost the one Jack gave me & want one.   Lew

To Philip Whalen, from Forks of Salmon, 14 *May* 1963

Dear Philip,   Yes, Rilke is very grim finally, but that is how it sounded then, in Europe, apparently, since all of them wrote that way. But it's sometimes good for me to read them, since I get too shrieky if I don't look out.

The weather is finally good! Rain, snow, cold, up until just a day or so ago. I got bit by a scorpeen who apparently wintered under my floorboards. I always wondered what it felt like. About half as bad as a bee.

Then I grubbed out some poison oak and came on with a very strange reaction: puffy, no itch, fever, red balls, eyes swollen almost shut, face and crotch on *fire*. I tried to talk to my cells and tell them their decision was foolish (and promising never to work with p.o. again). Today all is much better. I hope this will be the last attack for the summer.

Someone said you had bad asthma this year. Are you over it? Is that why you moved to S.F.?

Tomorrow I go give myself up to the Forestry. I don't mind at all. I'm tired of thinking and writing and reading and studying my ballistic tables. I don't have a single line of poetry in me & I'm glad.

It all goes into folders until I get another fit. I can't fix that big one at all, though I think if I do as Horace said it will be all written when next I look at it (maybe in 7 months—7 years is too long, as H's work proves—maybe in 7 weeks).

I want to work on a trail crew so I can learn something about handling stock, throwing the Diamond, and so I can see more of this country. I hope they don't offer me a lookout job, I am so tired of our friend Lewie.

What I want to do is save up enough to winter in S.F. for 2 or so months, anyway. Maybe I could eventually get layed. I seem to remember it is a pleasant exercise, both for the body & the soul.

All my hair is cut off.

Today I took my gold-pan out and worked and worked. I found some beautiful pyrite crystals ("Iron Pirates" as they are called here), but no gold. It is very pleasant work. You dunk sandwiches in the cold creek & watch mink drink. I'm going to build a portable sluice box so I can really "move dirt" as they say.

I'm glad to hear that your book is still on & sad to hear that Michael's is now a mess of scars (as Scaliger said). Tell him that Uncle Jack has told us and told us how to write novels & that what he should do is wrap up the first version (without even reading it) and send it off at once, everywhere.

Jack Boyce sends his regards. He bought 15 volumes of our writing & says that W C Williams still swings harder than anybody, but that you are more instructive. He accuses me of mesmerizing folks when I read out loud (forgetting all the chemicals and auras he'd stuffed himself with that and subsequent and previous evenings). Also, he finally smeared himself all over that big canvas he's been staring at all winter, & has even stretched another! A nice big square of exactly 6 feet every way. And has also nearly decided for sure to go to Japan and sit on his head. All of which pleases me since he was in quite a blind rage not so long ago & was stomping all over his toes.

Ron L[oewinsohn] returned the poem I gave him & said there won't be any *Change* in S.F.

Oh Yes! Despite the fact that you tease me all the time about Marianne Moore, I sent her a copy of *Wobbly Rock* (I always meant to, & hastened to do it on my return since the copies are almost all gone) & she wrote back a nice little card that said; "Very exact Mr. Welch

WOBBLY ROCK, my thanks."

But what really *happened* was, the card was a P.O. self-stamped job for TWO cents! And had been printed with her Brooklyn address on the back. I've been trying to figure when post cards were 2 cents & figure it must have been at least pre-War II & have a perfect image of that house and her in it (like that Sargent portrait with the dark light just coming through the inside shutters).

I hope your novel is better than those of Balzac. I have nothing but him to read & can't take it anymore. As you say, they just don't *swing*!

In case I never offered, please feel free to come up here any time you feel like it. If I get on trail, I'll be gone 10 days & here 4, there will be lots of food, and maybe you could work on a fire, even. I could pick you up in Yreka, or maybe somebody might like to take the drive.   yrs.   Lew

[P.S.] Today I thot I *smelled* a deer & looked up & sure enough, a doe was tiptoeing by my shack about 30 yards away

Change was a short-lived literary magazine edited by Richard Brautigan and Ron Loewinsohn.

To Kirby Doyle, from Forks of Salmon, 16 *May* 1963

Dear Kirby,   Get a new typewriter ribbon at once. They are coppable.

I am typing on my porch. A snake crawled under the stoop. I hope he eats all my mice. Wasps everywhere. They apparently spend their whole lives building nests so that new wasps can spend their whole lives building nests so that . . .

(VIZ, cab-vision, Welch, circa 1960: "The Universe is a vast cab company whose only passengers are drivers going to and from work.")

The one enduring image of our giant reading was that breakfast at Holly's: her son's eloquent "naming-of-the-toys" & her own incomparable "stoned-dance-of-peppercorns." I fell hopelessly in love with her (more so, even, than when I first saw her dance at Nepenthe on a sunny afternoon several years ago). Did she have her new baby? I am jealous of you & sad for me. Tell her I have a hard-on for her 400 miles long.

And that I'll bring my chain saw and axe and buck her winter's wood ONLY if she stops messing around with unreliable types like you.

What is she doing in Larkspeare? What news? I demand precise account of my Beatrice!

•

I have poison oak very strangely. It doesn't so much itch as burn. I swell, rather than blister. Fever (slight). Nightmares (sad). I'm going to stop this for a while and pan for gold.

•

I actually found gold! For days I've been panning and panning & never found anything but maybe some black sand (a good sign) until I was sure I was doing it all wrong, but then I looked real close and there it was, gold! 3 specks about like fly specks, very thin flake-gold. I figure 14,000,000 ought to make up into an ounce.

It sure is fun though. You poke around taking samples of dirt in old river beds (you can tell because all the rocks are worn round) and then you wash it and whirl it and pretty soon there's only this little scum of black sand. Meanwhile the creek is pretty (I'm working on my own claim by God!) and today a deer came down and drank & saw me and jumped straight up in the air and floundered around in the creek like crazy. The water is real cold and you get all hypnotized watching the water spin the gravel in the pan.

I'm not writing right now either, & I'm glad. Tired of my mind my poems myself.

Applied for Forestry work yesterday & hope to get on a trail crew. But it looks like I'll end up at the guardhouse at the Forks on standby for fires. Easier, but not as much fun or dough.

I want to save enough to spend at least 2 months in S.F. next winter. It was ok here last winter, even necessary, but I am tired of being alone so much. And I hear that there's not a budget from Uncle until July, so maybe I'll have to find something else to do next month. I have $1.68 to me name. But food.

I think you're very brave, or foolish, or both, even to *consider* L.A. It's an evil place, even when there are lots of groovy friends. Everyone is out of bread down there & everyone is just about to get a $600 a week job. People die on the freeways. All movies are now made in Europe. Liz Taylor gets $2,000,000 for showing ⅞ths of her abnormally swollen tits while wearing a Cleo wig. 10,000 musicians

114

(great ones, some) are out of work. Writers try to write fake pornography in order to live. There is smog all summer—your eyes water and you sneeze & gasp. In the canyons, one is always in danger of being burned to death in 100 mph brush fires. Even the phonies are phony phonies. As I once wrote:

> Fucked LA starlet of tiny dreams untrue even to your
> tiny dreams . . .

But you know all this. (Dig, there are also thousands of Mulottoes, naked to the waist, who practice looking like what they understand to be, they think, a sullen Angel. I understand you have to have, or pretend to have, a cock 11½'' long & 5 bongo drums to do this right.)

Everyone wears sandals and sandals ruin your feet.

But go, Tully, go if you must. Don't say I didn't warn you.   Lew

[P.S.] Yes, Love. Perhaps it can even defeat L.A. I, however, would hear the sinister sad sound of all those millions even if Venus herself were fondling me in my bedroom. I think it's maybe because the bedroom has Venetian blinds.

I spent years 3, 4, & 5 in a little stucco house in Santa Monica. My brain is still scarred by it. There was a tile-top "coffee table" in the living room. My mother made me wear high shoes & short pants to kindergarten. The "Gypsys" stole my trike. In helpless frustration I used to urinate all over the clothes in my own closet. [On envelope:] Jack [Boyce] made big beautiful painting & has new 6' × 6' stretched and sends warmest etc.

To Lew Welch, from Marianne Moore, 260 Cumberland Street, Brooklyn, 25 May 1963

Yes, Mr. Welch, I am for squeek—"Shack Simple" *most* therapeutic.

You've raised my spirits. Sorry I have to leave you for (as it may seem, like) for good. —am beset by "civilization" of every known variety: by nature, "private."!

No hiding-place, is there?   M.M.

Dear Joanne, How nice to get your beautiful card. The picture of Mt. Aso is very fine. Yes, Nemi [Frost] & P[hilip] Lamantia made a big scene but it wasn't over vodka. P. began screaming and we all thought he couldn't stop. Then Nemi had some kind of tantrum so Mike M[cClure] had to leave early. Don Allen left even before all that & the main poem I wanted everybody to hear did not fit on the tape recorder, and it wasn't finished anyway so I had to make the last part up. I don't know what I said, but everyone cheered and cheered. Then I got back here and read it. It seems to be about somebody almost dying of some kind of longing. There are vows. It is all very confusing.

Kirby and I were very boxed after nearly 10 days of preparation, he in the middle of losing Dee, and great hospitality from everybody. We blew far too hard and too long & had Monk and Coleman on the phonograph with Shannon [Doyle] as d.j. We wanted to transport everybody on great shouts of love and glee & apparently did so. But since then I can't even look at my poems or the inside of my head.

Neither can Kirby.

Now to answer yr. questions. Yes, I am sure rocks live. Somebody (I can't find who) wrote a beautiful poem about how it is to be a rock. There are terrible pressures and temperatures. At the end the crystals are proof that the whole point was to be beautiful. Especially if you have the time to be an agate.

The same goes for adjectives. They are real whenever they are. Ginsberg is the master of adjectives, he makes nouns out of them ("angelheaded hipster" . . . "negro streets"). Duncan says "hurt voluptuous grace," making something very weird. I use adjectives as seldom as possible.

I don't know how to become *how,* either. I'll think about that.

If [Stan] Persky said they were unimpressed by *your* poetry, I think you should know that Phil W[halen] was most impressed & he is harder to impress than anyone. So was I, also by the beautiful Indian rubbings. If you mean that Persky was unimpressed (together with his "they") with *my* poetry, I don't care.

After thinking and thinking all winter long I think I am finally becoming almost able to realize in what sense it is all Mind. Everybody but me seems to know this. Eddington (astronomer/physicist): *the world is made of "Mind-Stuff." Of course I don't mean mind or stuff, but you know what Mind is.* Mr. Garlan, the Reed philosopher whom you met, told me to "give up your X world. You've already said you can't see it or speak it or know it. As long as you pretend it's there you'll be very lonely." The next day I was surprised and delighted by the way the highway straightened itself out as it rolled beneath my car. But today (now) I feel like I'm living in a big green cloud of my own making & I'm very nervous about what might be outside (it).

The real answer is I am stupid and able to spin words any way I like. Also there is a vast con-game going on & I can't see why it's necessary. If I even think about it, I get sick.

Here is what I am doing. Lizards. Wasps. Every day a thunder-shower. Muggy heat. 6 green snakes ate all my frogs. Poison oak. Trout with orange and blue spots. Ice in small lakes. Naked all day long. Crew cut. 5 tomato plants. A small black bear. [. . .] love, Lew

"the main poem": Welch is describing his and Kirby Doyle's reading of his "Din Poem" at the Batman Gallery in San Francisco in May.

To Jack Kerouac, from Forks of Salmon, 20 June 1963

Dear Jack,   Are you still drinking and d-r-r-r-r-r-r-inking? I've decided not to drink on Tuesdays.

Also I never wear any clothes, now that it's summer. This little CCC shack is across the river (literally and in all senses) & nobody ever comes over on this side, so there's nobody to be offended by the sight of my hairy red balls, so why not?

It is hot and muggy. Thunderheads build up all the time and thunder mutters, and even though I'm supposed to be on "stand-by" for forest fires they never call me up. Soon it will be July, though, and maybe they'll hire me steady (the Forestry) & I can save up enough money to spend next winter in S.F. or New York. One more winter in this shack & I'll be nuttier than Han Shan. Which maybe is ok.

This is now a world of lizards and butterflies. Six green snakes ate all my frogs. I saw a little bear cub with such a *very* shiny new black coat. When you walk thru the fields tiny grasshoppers spray out in all directions from your feet. I fill 2 tubs with water every morning & by afternoon the sun has heated it just right & I bathe in one and rinse in the other by dumping it over my head.

The other day a batch of brothers (Faulknerian, like his good guys, that is) and I dug a grave for an illegitimate & premature baby. It had only weighed 2½ lbs. and only "lived" about 2 hours, and one of the brothers was responsible, and they felt it should receive proper burial since it *did* live for a while. So we dug a hole in almost solid rock, using a quart of Old Overholt & four big sticks of dynamite.

No matter how I try, the huge agonized face of all victimized humanity, tyrant & slave of every place and time, looks down at me from the cabin wall—a movie stuck on a single frame. There is no use making it dissolve into its individuals—all you get that way is a stack of atrocity stories, each as unnecessary & pointless & appalling as the next. And, shadowed over this Face, so that both images are one, is this nice little green planet, exactly fitted to our size. the Face speaks. It says: "All right buddy, C'mere." . . . "Where's your ID?" . . . "How long you lived at that address?" . . . "Get in the car."

What do your blue eyes see? love, Lew

P.S.: I have a crew cut & look like a long bony old major league ballplayer name of Cy Thompson or maybe C. T. Blaine.

To Donald Allen, from Forks of Salmon, 27 June 1963

Dear Don, Forgive me for not answering your beautiful warm letter until now. I kept hoping I'd have the long poem in shape to show you. But it just won't get done. It isn't a "poetic" problem, it's just that I can't understand what the damned thing is trying to say.

Maybe it's too ambitious. Maybe the form I conceive is incorrect. It seems to want to say everything & not to be satisfied until it has. I keep pecking away at it. Many very lovely new sections.

Yes, next time we'll have to keep away from the booze and the table (which I finally realize is your work-desk & that often when I visit you you've been reading and reading all day & are exhausted). It would be fun to go on a picnic with boxes full of those Chinese dainties, perhaps some cold sake, drunk from bowls, & while away the afternoon beneath trees, by the edge of a stream, with a fog blowing in. I know just the place.

If ever you feel like it, please feel free to visit me. There is plenty of room & the country is beautiful. Someone said you have a VW.

Is that true?

I'll be working, I hope, starting July 1st. My mother will visit Monday, I don't know for how long. Even if I'm working you could take over the place during the day, take walks, go fishing. It is very restful.

I hope to be able to save enough to spend at least a few months, this winter, in S.F. Another winter here will make me as kooky as Han Shan & I'm not sure I want that yet.

Attached are my "Early Summer" poems. I am not quite as sad as they are—am mostly like numbers 2 & 3. On the other hand, I seem to be finally "growing up." Alas.   love,   Lew

[P.S.] The title of the group is perhaps too disrespectful?

"After Chinks" was the title of the group of poems.

To Kirby Doyle, from Forks of Salmon, 20 July 1963

Dear Kirby,   Word has it that you're indeed in L.A. & had a reading & are being lionized and that everything is all right. But I worry.

As you well know I am world's welterweight worry champ & all I know is that your last letter had 11 counts of bad in it, any one of which would wipe me out. In addition I vaguely remember what I wrote to you & what I remember was full of self-pity & lacking in love and compassion. Forgive me. All is not well with me. Often, I fail.

I miss you terribly. What news?

I tried to write you in my usual fashion, giving you what was on my mind right now, but I destroyed it. It was exactly like the letters in *Miss Lonelyhearts.* You know, "Dear Miss L., I lost my nose..." etc.

I haven't lost my nose. Actually everything is ok. It is only that my mother has been here in this little cabin for 3 weeks and I have been horrid to her. My sister is going to have a leg amputated, almost surely. There is no money. The Forestry is accidentally? preventing me from working. I am terrified.

Dan Wann keeps me alive simply by being the fantastic Bodhisattva he is. Now and then I stick my head in the spring.

I had a big rush of poetry 4 weeks ago (12 poems). One was for you & I attach it with deepest most heartfelt love. Please write.
Lew

[Enc.] "The Live Museum"

To Philip Whalen, from Forks of Salmon [Summer 1963?]

Phil,

   "I can't do anything unless I've got some place that I can sit down comfortably." [*You Didn't Even Try*, p. 142.]

   Here is example of (to my ear) the "floating that." I hear need for "in" or "on" after comfortably—but that only says something about my ear,
               you, several people of all kinds, use the structure.
   Thanks for letting me read your beautiful novel.   Lew

To Donald Allen, from Forks of Salmon, 20 August 1963

Dear Don,   I finished them. It takes so long to get them right—6 days fussing over 3 little poems.
   "After Chinks" of course all wrong—consider it a private joke.
   Use "Early Summer Hermit Song" for broadside.
   "Hiking Poem" was published, wrong, in *Foot.* "marching" for "merging," "sack" for "pack," horrible errors in spacing for a poem whose form is a shape: it is visual, ruined by cramped packing and bad printing. Also it is not strong enough for your fine new mag., or maybe I just think of it as awfully long ago.
   These I attach are the best parts of "Spring Rain Revolution at the Forks," now a book, originally conceived as a neat 6 part poem, but after what I heard myself reading in April now utterly changed. All lies & rhetoric removed, no money ranting, a book of smaller poems held more loosely together, each poem tighter.
   I think I've found the big Western sound in "Big Chevvy Engine Song" & "Live Museum." It is also in "Songs from Rat Flat" & (now titled) "Early Summer Hermit Songs."
   These last, by the way, I only sent for your amusement. Do you think *ER* might want them? If so, ok, but I want to pick at them (you'll see how different the one I send is from what the first poem was).
   And what is *ER* doing with "Rat Flat"? Shall I bug them? I want $200 for "Songs in RF." McClure got that for dope essays.
   Right now I'm working 7 days a week & can't hardly do more than come home, eat, wash dishes, & go to sleep. But the winter grubstake looks almost certain. I was in a real panic.

How I wish I could be in S.F. to see Allen & Charles & hear them read etc.

Your mag. ought to be called Big West, Edge, Last Coast, or Drop Off, to indicate what it is: the last shriek from a people who have gone West so far they are now in the East or drowned.

It is all over, but we choose to keep on speaking.

> I cannot think of anyone who is or
> was or will be living who I envy.
> A bear was *in my cabin* 5 days ago!
> I'll shoot the varmit

Lew

P.S. I have carbons of all attached. Will you have time to send me proofs? I promise instant return.

"After Chinks," "Songs from Rat Flat," and "Early Summer Hermit Songs" are all earlier titles for what eventually became *Hermit Poems*. "Big Chevvy Engine Song" and "Live Museum" became poems in "The Way Back" series. The "new mag." underwent a metamorphosis and became the Writing Series.

To Philip Whalen, from Forks of Salmon, 15 September 1963

Dear Phil,   Pls. excuse my silence. I work all the time w/no days off almost ever & can't seem to write anybody. Is your novel done? I imagine you're having gaudy (gawdy) nites & days w/Allen? Saw your good review of his book. I continue to find a poem now & then. Very plain right now. What news? Turkey shoot today.

Raining.   Lew

To Kirby Doyle, from Forks of Salmon, 14 October 1963

Kirby,   Are you still out of gaol?

I read your lovely high letter to Jack B[oyce], who is now somewhere East and trying, I suspect, to get back West.

He said he was going to tell you to send the parcel to me, since if you send it to him he won't be there and it will sit and sit. Perhaps sprout?

If it is cooler to send railway express do so, since our postman is also an expressman & there would be no hang-up.

I imagine what with the Series & all that you do not have minute one for any real business. You guys must have really cleaned up, unless, as I imagine, all the folks got loyal and backed up the Dodgers. A balanced load would have been very dandy.

I am seriously considering making my Chevvy into a modest rod. Sparkle-green, tough discs, smittys. It is, I now realize & have been droolingly told by car-wild Indians on this river, a cherry '54!

I now have a pair of cruel boots for city wear. Also a black jacket with Swiss blue lining that will not quit.

You said that some L.A. dancing chick wanted to write to me. Why didn't, doesn't, she? Tell her to write me dirty letters. I will answer in kind. We can tell each other exactly what we'll do to every square inch of each other when we meet.

I have this huge mountain load and lots of brand new money.

As near as I can see, this work will end about November 1st. Then I'll get my wood in, put in 3 new windows, lay new linoleum on the floor, pack my car, and come to San Francisco

400 miles through valleys of larks   love,   Lew

To David Haselwood and Andrew Hoyem, from Forks of Salmon,
20 November 1963

Dear Auerhahns,   As the Dharma would have it, I decided only yesterday to quit my job and be in S.F. by Monday, so all is already ready.

Yes, I will definitely be able to read on the 26th.

I only got yr. letter today, Wednesday. I will try to phone you tonite. If that fails, I'll mail this tonite at the store (where the phone is, 8 miles away).

I only get mail Mon. Wed. Fri., so if I wait till Friday you wouldn't get this letter till Monday. Whenever possible, please try to get info to me in time to include 4 days (2 coming & 2 going. I am very far away).

And very tired. And lonely. And delighted to hear of your reading, which will stand as the wow beginning to a winter's freedom at last. love to you, and all   soon   Lew

122

To Henry Rago, from 382 *Shoreline Highway, Mill Valley,*
15 *December* 1963

Dear Mr. Rago,   I enclose a group of poems for your consideration.

I've published in *Evergreen Review, S.F. Review, Contact,
Nomad, Chicago Review* (1952), and have 2 poems in the Grove
anthology, *New American Poetry* etc., and have had several read-
ings here in San Francisco, the latest being a big bash with the
Auerhahn poets & Allen Ginsberg—about 2 weeks ago. *Wobbly
Rock*, Auerhahn, is my 1 book.

I've just returned from more than a year's hermitage in the
mountains of California.

The enclosed poems are part of the large book I wrote last year.
Two sections of the long poem which is the main part of this book
will appear in Don Allen's new magazine, "New Review."

Don has acted for many years as my agent and editor, and it is at
his suggestion that I send you this work. For some reason I don't
understand, *Evergreen* keeps refusing my poems. Don is also
confused as to why. And I would like to branch out, now, into less
wild publishing areas. Not only that, I'm broke.

My compliments to you for the more exciting magazine *Poetry*
has recently become, and hoping you'll find these poems usable. I
am, etc.   Lew Welch

1964

To Henry Rago, from 382 *Shoreline Highway, Mill Valley,*
1 *February* 1964

Dear Mr. Rago, Your acceptance of my poems brought about
the most productive days I've had in several months. Thank you. I
had not realized how badly I needed something to get me off my
ass.

Yes, you may renumber the poems as you suggest.

I enclose the form. Please note the address c/o my mother—her
address is far more stable than mine. I promise swift attention to
proofs.

I don't have a suitable picture. Fred McDarrah, in N.Y., has
some pictures of me for the meantime, & I'll send one for your files
whenever.

Please change the title of the group to "From, The Hermit
Songs."

· · · · · · · · · ·

"The Hermit Songs," it now appears, will be a group of about 20
short lyrics. Originally I saw them divided into 4 seasons, but now
don't want to break them up that way. The 4 you have chosen will
be the end of the group (perhaps with the insertion of a poem or
two, but surely ending with "Ring of Bone").

Most of these songs come easily, as a relief, a bonus, a compres-
sion, or whatever, as I work through the difficulties of a long poem
now called "Spring Rain Revolution at the Forks."

This last work seems to want to be nearly 50 pages long. Struc-
turally, it will move like *Paterson* (that is, looser than *The Cantos*)
but tighter than *Paterson* (I am not trying a river)—each unit is a
nearly separate poem. Some units only 8 lines long, some 4 or 5
pages.

No titles, no numbers, & a blur of the idea of series. Where each
unit reads as a word in a long sentence, finally, if I succeed. White
space will be used as a positive music—as in Monk's jazz.

The poem is "about" exile and return. Describes a year of mine in the woods, last year, during which I tried to figure out in terms of everything—starting with the fact at hand: the oatmeal, the woodstove, the piss can, Avalokiteshvara, the essential shuck, the basic con, tyrant and slave of every place and time, my own loneliness.

I am not succeeding in doing all this. The poem rages into rhetoric, says the "thing that is not so," and regularly appears to me as a work of the wrong kind of derangement.

Further, I don't know how the Songs fit in. They may work into the main texture of the poem. They may sit as Rilke's *Sonnets* to his *Elegies* (certainly the process of their composition is the same).

Yesterday, I decided to stop the whole thing, be satisfied with the Songs, forget it. Today I don't know.

It is sometimes unfortunate to have a need to structure too far. On the other hand, that is the way the mind does work. How much easier it would be if the big structure were, say, the 100 sonnets of a sequence. Then, when a sonnet gets made it just adds on to the others & finally it's all done.

The way our forms are, it is never possible to know where you are until it is all done. It should be "blown" at one sitting, like jazz, but my energies are not up to that.

· · · · ·

To answer the "Additional information" part of the form: I've applied for a job teaching Indian kids in Alaska next winter.

I am now unemployable here in the U.S. & there are many satisfying things about the Alaska teaching job—not the least of which is the fact that I'll end up with $3,000 or so in real American dollars.

I intend to spend that wad by going to Japan & then around the world, backwards. I've never been out of the States because of extreme poverty.

Thank you again for your interest in my work.

Joanne Snyder, nee Kyger, is now back in the States (Gary will be here within a month). She is, I am sure, the best lady poet working. I will try to get her to send you some of her poems. But I think if you wrote her a letter asking for them it might be easier for her. She needs, right now, encouragement. Please don't tell her I said so.

She can be reached c/o Philip Whalen, 123 Beaver St., S.F.
Lew Welch

"Spring Rain Revolution at the Forks" became "The Way Back."

125

To Katharine George (at Forks of Salmon),
from 382 *Shoreline Highway, Mill Valley,* 11 *February* 1964

Dear Katharine & all Georges,   I just wrote [Ted] Bordon in
Alaska a letter to get things started.

Either I am nutty as everybody else is down here, or it doesn't
bother me so much anymore. Anyway, I feel more or less at ease,
finally. How are things with you?

I used up all my money already, but about $200 of it was used to
get a couple I know off the hook (a story too complicated to go
into), and now he is making big money as some kind of petty hood-
lum & will be able to pass me a "dime" ($10) or even a "4-bit piece"
($50) now and then until we are square. I tried to get the Unemploy-
ment thing started, but had such a hangover the day of my appointment that I had to chicken out, phone, and make a new one—next
Thursday.

All other money-tries have failed.

I placed nearly 50 pages of poetry here and there, but you don't
get paid at all, usually, and when you do you get paid on date of
publication—which is sometimes 6 months later. Altogether I have
about $30 coming in somewhere or other.

However, I am now so famous I am very likely immortal. Isn't
that strange?

Also, there is a fine dinner party almost every night. Much free
liquor. Good talk.

This place I live in has turned into such a circus (almost never
less than 8 or 10 folks raging in and out, singing, talking, et al.) that
I seldom really live here—even though I'm paid up for more than a
month. My mail, however, should still be sent to this address.

So many folks have 2 houses or are gone all day or over week-
ends, that I can successfully camp out at various locations: here a
day, there a week, etc. If all this, for any reason, sounds wild, free,
and exciting, FORGET IT! It mainly is very tiring and time-consum-
ing and hectic. I long for a quiet, sunny, little room where I can
lock the door and get some work done.

None of it makes any sense at all, and I keep wondering why I
don't come back to the river. But then I have to admit I don't *want*
to, right now. Why, I don't know, but you have to be true to that
kind of certain feeling, or you crash.

No doubt the whole hang-up is chicks—of which there are thousands of more or less satisfactory lays and not one good love-shot

you'd really like to have in the house all the time. Or maybe I'm just getting to be a cranky old bachelor.

As soon as some of this stuff gets into print, I'll send you copies.

Tell Tom I've decided to take a plain old Model 70 .338 Magnum to Alaska. He was right. A .35 Whelen is just too complicated.

Has Dave got any further with his Methodist Creek deal? It is hard for me to imagine why I should work that hard, now, when all I do is rage around, get drunk, talk talk talk, and still manage to stay fed warm and dry—but finally I'll crash,   surely?

On the other hand I may limp back your way, thin and disgusted, any day.   my love to you all,   Lew

To Henry Rago, from 503 *West Blithedale, Mill Valley,*
31 *May* 1964

Dear Mr. Rago,   I finally have a fairly permanent address—will be here for at least 6 months: 503 West Blithedale, Mill Valley, California.

Gary Snyder is back from Japan for a while & we have organized a giant reading as per the attached. The hall is the funky old place where Harry Bridges won the coast & has a monstrous mural (very well done) showing policemen beating women and children to death—the fuzz mounted on horses with hooves like Percherons, which hooves are crushing the heads of brave men etc. Nobody knows who painted it. When we asked: "Nobody knows. Except it was some Wobbly lady from Seattle."

S.F. and the Bay Area grow more responsive to poetry every day. Gary, Phil and I have been on the radio (FM), the *Chronicle* loves us (maybe a whole column by Ralph Gleason, local jazz column writer & very good man), everyone very excited. I predict 1,000 souls.

"You guys come on like scholars. No shit, for a long time I thought you were putting us on, like maybe you were a road cast from *Evergreen* or something, the real Lew Welch in the woods, Snyder still in Japan, Whalen safe and hiding."

This from the man at KPFA (FM) after our interview & indicative of the general problem & cause for real hope.

General Problem: big fear/hate thing called war between hip & square. Poet seen as frightening hippydip. Incommunicable (poets!) folks who mumble, snarl, etc. etc.

Cause for Real Hope: All folks delighted by actual article. Express huge need for Poetry. Prove this by quick pickup of the poems (in this town you can hardly get a 50 line structure out, out loud, for interference of shrieks of laughter, cheers, etc.).

For all the reasons we all know (and which, I say, we must forget —no blame, as *I Ching* says) the whole thing got hopelessly fucked up. Ginsberg in N.Y. beautifully correcting things. We 3 (and dozens of others) here in S.F. also putting it right. Or trying to.

And, weirdly, all this is happening without any real change in approach. The poems are actually tougher. I wear long hair and black boots. Why not? I'm handsome and vain. Snyder has a beard, patched jeans, a wild little over-the-shoulder black Jap bag thing. Of course! Poets have to carry books, mss., all manner of clumsy articles. Whalen wears funky old overall-type jeans, immaculately clean, simply because he's portly & can't make it in Levi's & he's poor, terribly poor . . . . . .

How to say anything without causing a new confusion. That's what actually went wrong. One answer. Write more. Write more accurately. Write tough.

Every time we cheat, even unknowingly, thousands "die of our cowardice."

How great to have our job at a time like this—Eh Henry? Lew Welch

[P.S.] Can't you figure a way to make this reading? Worth it. Also, June in S.F. unbelievable. Try.   LW

[Enc. Handbill for the 12 June reading.]

The "man at KPFA": Jack Nessel, who moderated and produced the *On Bread & Poetry* panel discussion.

To Donald Allen, from 503 *West Blithedale, Mill Valley,*
8 *July* 1964

Dear Don,   I enclose the "Hermit Songs, " "I Fly Out," and 3 Leo Poems as promised, on time.

Also "Song to a Secret Farm," which I mean only as a gift to Creeley, in respect for his craft. Print it, though, if you & he want to, of course.

Wobbly Rock and the "Hermit Songs" show only part of my voice, some of my meters, etc. If you can, I want very much to have my wilder voices shown. I suffer, sometimes, from a plain-ness—spring out of that, often—want to show it.

Writing this letter makes me realize I want to attach, also, "Dane Poem" (written last week) and "How Strange It Is to Know" (1964).

Maybe "I Fly Out" will fit into your prose section? I don't see any difference between prose and poetry anymore, except ab-stractly, and I think most of us think that way. I suppose some fancy poles exist, but I don't think about them, writing, and don't know of anyone who does. And "Man Who Played Himself" will confuse the squares unless other things went along with it, and I have no more "prose." Is "October in the Railroad Earth" prose? Who cares.

"I Fly Out" might help somebody get out. I know that Sherwood Anderson's way of splitting from Chicago—a folk tale only, I be-lieve, that is, did he write it?—has helped spring thousands. It is known all over Chicago. "Someday, I'll pull a Sherwood Anderson," they say. And some do.

Please send Creeley the carbon of this letter. For a long time I've wanted to correspond, meet, etc.

Hi Bob!   yours, Don   Lew

Welch had been invited to contribute to *The New Writing in the USA*, which Penguin Books was to publish in 1967. The biographical note in the following letter was for the same anthology. "October in the Railroad Earth"—by Jack Kerouac.

To Donald Allen, from Mill Valley, 17 *September* 1964

Don—Apologies for long delay. I am at my wit's end, again. Can't seem to get the simplest thing done. Forgive me. It will change as it always does. Gasp.   Lew

LEW WELCH
Born August 16, 1926, sign of Leo, to tragically typical Lost Gener-ation, bad booze, biggish money, parents, in Phoenix, Arizona—then the town of President Hoover, Frank Luke, the Goldwaters, all personal friends of my family. I never really knew my father, a roaring 20s/depression casualty, now dead. Grew up with my mother and sister in dozens of little California towns, never in one place 3 years. I made it, then, by running fast (49.8, once, in the 440, in high school) and by pretending not to be too bright. Air Force, World War II. No combat. 7 years in universities, all over

the U.S., on G.I. Bill. B.A. from Reed College. Crack up, psycho-analysis, advertising, in Chicago, till 1958. Since then a precarious existence in mountains and San Francisco, turning a buck however I may, trying not to be bitter, trying to get at my work. You cannot do good work, in America, if you are *in any way* affiliated with *anything*. Naturally gregarious and joyful, it's been hard for me to accept this truth. I keep crashing against it. "Yes" is the answer. Yes. And keep on coming back.

To Dorothy Brownfield, after a visit to her Verano, California, home in 1964

Thanx for the roast and
    Sunday—
Watched your view thru
    acacia, phone lines, goal
    posts, houses & (miraculously)
        cows!

That bank of hills steams
    like Peru, or we might
as well be in Africa—

Notice how the live oaks on
    our round California hills
      browse,
Like buffalo

I return to teeming lives

1965

To Bill Deemer, from 123 *Beaver Street, San Francisco,*
23 *March* 1965

Dear Bill,   Thanx for the poems, they are far better than the last
ones you sent. In fact they are so good I now
    Seat myself upon my Roshi pillow, tie meseff up in my puce belt
(given in jest to me by my master when he sent me off as hopelessly . . .) and for whatever use:
    Postcard poem should be titled "Postcard 400 Miles Long" &
then begin as you do, and go as it goes. Except maybe "1 will mail
this tomorrow" etc? I.e. keep it all a postcard? Yes, I think so.
    My most extravagant praises for . . . "birds I'll bet along the
fence brush." Very fine. Excellent.
II. Kim Novak Poem is perfect.
III. "For Laura Lee" also, very beautiful. I'd take out "as from a
dream" for reasons metrical and because of sense-speed. Why "as
you *had* left it" & not just "as you left it." Bothers my ear, unless
you read it "you'd" (which is ugly yewed). Suit yourself.
IV. "A Different Kind of Daffodil"
(The real reason for this teacher-shot)
The poem goes as in the first version. The second version received
today is no good. It is not good, Bill. Watch. The poem is:

> This is not Sebastopol but I think of daffodils—
> there is one in a coke bottle on my desk—
>   that hurried you down the road to meet me
> for I held flowers.
>
> My hand was sweet with sap for days.
>   (end)

This is so beautiful and right it makes me cry.
    But the business of "The words I write to you / are perennials
within our heart / etc." no. NO! That's explainy-blather—means "I
am a poet" in a wrong way, not for example, as in your printed

poem: ". . . invoke you/ as a temple will, in/ gravel beeswax/ plum tree."

I figure you got drunk with music. "The roadside daffodils outside Sebastopol" is very heady and wild. I know, really I do know, what got you all hung up. It is fun, right, is really where your ear is (it's extraordinarily good, your ear)—what a relief, by the way, since most stuff nowadays is all Johnny-one-note. Thunk.

But. Don't ever tell a girl the words you write have syllables of golden bells, not even if she has a tin ear. Which she don't. All you get that way is never layed.

Spin her the syllables easy like and fast and there she is all wet with love and can't figure out how
spinning her head it was
you said all that?

So, it goes:

ROADSIDE DAFFODILS OUTSIDE SEBASTOPOL

This is not Sebastopol but I think of daffodils—
there is one in a coke bottle on my desk—
    that hurried you down the road to meet me
for I held flowers.

My hand was sweet with sap for days.

This way, she, She, knows what the sap was, gets drunk on your syllables, comes back again and again. For more.

Don't ever show Her this letter.

It is for us to really know how daffodil/sebastopol/outside/roadside works, our trade you might say, what we diddle with over a beer, leering, longing. But never crack.

It's a Mystery!   (we hear from her & don't explain)   Lew

To Robert Hawley, from 123 *Beaver Street, San Francisco,*
20 *June* 1965

Dear Bob,   At Dave Meltzer's suggestion, I attach a ms. of poems for your consideration.

Some of them date back to the mid-fifties, some are new, some have perhaps been already *overexposed* (as certain types have said) in readings, magazines, and anthologies, and some are new (were put in just now to clarify the shape of the book).

But I think the book has coherence, and am very anxious to get it printed, to have it stand as a first selected works.

It has been mostly my own insecurity & my own bewilderment about the publishing world, that has held these poems up this long. For bewilderment read "periodic despair."

I don't really understand, and certainly don't approve of, whatever jockeying of power seems to be going on right now, but from what I've heard of you, and from what I've seen of Oyez, it looks like you are properly aloof from most, or all, of it. I just want to get these poems printed, by anyone who can do it, and who wants to do it because they like the poems.

As you probably know, I am in that Berkeley Poetry Conference, reading July 24th, so if you're interested in doing this book, I think you could probably get some of your investment back fairly quickly, if it's at all possible to have the book printed by that time. I have almost nothing in print right now. The Auerhahn Society will do my Hermit Poems (8 short lyrics) very beautifully by then, but that will be about all.

Congratulations on the good job you did for Meltzer.   yours very truly, Lew Welch

Oyez published this ms, *On Out*, that year, and Four Seasons Foundation published the *Hermit Poems.*

To Lew Welch, from Richard Brautigan, San Francisco,
26 July 1965

Dear Lew,   I got a new ribbon today, so I thought that I would write you a letter about a certain poet named Lew Welch who is mentioned favorably on page 236 in *The Literary Rebel* written by Kingsley Widmer and published by the Southern Illinois University Press.

It is also rumored that the same poet can walk on water. I can't remember the distance. Life in the 20th Century is so hectic. Say hello to Philip.   Yours,   Richard

Thank you, Lew Welch, for seeing a reason to mention me. You say compactly, some things I've always wanted to say.
    I recognize, like as much as ever,
        "His color faded with his life. A small green fish"

In *On Out* I like:

       even an idiot could understand

       Fern   Trees

       a small brown bird
       actual berries from my hand

       WOBBLY ROCK; even a good gust of wind will do it

       I used to watch the Pelican

       where the cat lept

       I rate my fury with the bumblebee

    I wish you happiness of your method. Like the picture
Marianne Moore
[P.S.] After a month, I'll be moved to 35 West Ninth Street 7B, N.York 11

1966

QUESTION MAN, BY O'HARA
[*San Francisco Chronicle,* 23 April 1966]

Question: Ever Fight with a Guy over a Girl?

Lew Welch, poet and ship's clerk: I been in fights but never over a girl. Guys fighting over girls is something girls dreamed up. Makes them feel good. They like the idea, I guess. Say she's flirting around. Just stay cool. Ignore her. That'll infuriate her. If she's dumb enough to be fooling around with another cat, let her go.

To James Schevill, from 52 *Buckelew Street, Marin City, California,* 5 *August* 1966

Dear Mr. Schevill,   Yes, I'd be delighted to read for you on October 26.

When I read for the [Poetry] Center (I think about 1959) I made a statement for the program note which always pleased me. I wrote it over the phone, from work, backed by the roar of the Bemis Bag factory, and it was a good clear statement of what I'm about, composing.

Do you have this on file? I've lost my copy.

Please send it to me so I can use it again as part of this reading's program note.

Also, I'll have photographs and publicity copy for you in ample time for the reading. As you know, I've given several local readings on my own, or underwritten by others, and have a large following in the Bay Area. You should expect from 3 to 5 hundred people at the Museum of Art.

I say this, not as a cocky boast, but because I don't want to disappoint my many friends—as has happened in the past—and I just can't read in those gloomy little side rooms in the Museyroom.

I promise you I'll fill that big center room in the Museum & the promise extends to assuming full responsibility for whatever extra costs. Ralph Gleason will give me a large part of his column on the preceding Monday. I also know how to get free articles, long ones, into the news part of the *Chronicle*. (Those tiny spaces among the atrocity reports.)

All this stems from the belief that the Poet must pay his way, and can, if given half a chance. You have given me that half a chance, as others have, and, as we did before, I'd like to go all the way with this.

My poetry speaks to a great many, and I finally learned, after learning to write right, how to get a great many there to hear it. The year I was crippled (1964) I appeared 47 times as a poet, read before a total of 12,000 people (a .290 average blown up, considerably, by the inclusion of those I taught—also on a noninstitutional, or "wildcat," basis), and made $2,184.00—not a worthwhile sum, considering the effort, but maybe a local, at least, record, and enough to keep me alive until my leg got out of its cast. That is, I did all this while crippled. Because I had to.

Of course, that year only showed me how much I need the help of people like you. It's impossible to work that way. It killed Mark Twain, and it nearly killed me.

But it did leave me with the kind of "chops," as the folks say, whereby I can now help you augment your no doubt dinky budget. Or, more than pay my way. Let's try it.

Let's put it on a less grim level than this letter seems to be. I'll bet you:

TERMS OF BET

I bet you a fifth of good whiskey I can get more than 300 people to hear me the night of October 26 at the S.F. Museum of Art.

If I fail, I'll pay the difference in cost between the gloomy little side room and the big one. (In addition to the 5th of whiskey, which, I stipulate, must be drunk by you and me and Mark [Linenthal] and whatever women we choose to bring along.)

FURTHER, I assume *all* responsibility for whatever embarrassments might occur. Like, you say, "The crazy megalomaniac wanted that room and only 5 folks showed up and I like to lose my job. Jesus!" And I'll say, "Jim is absolutely right. I blew it!" I'll even say this in print.

AND STILL FURTHER, I agree to meet whatever extra financial demand IN FRONT! That is, your generous $200 gives me the room

to dip into my finally pretty good money from working on the
waterfront to make it certain that I

will not read in those gloomy little side rooms as Duncan did.
(The big room is weird enough!)

.   .   .

Jim, I know all the foregoing sounds like a promo-man's act, not
like a poet's acceptance of a generous offer, an offer I really appreciate, because I'm tired.

I can say the above to you because I know your work and therefore know that the usual bullshit need not apply. I.e., you are yourself a poet, a good one, and we need not talk about that.

But maybe now we do, because of my above hard-conning
(maybe) letter.

All the foregoing babble is nonpoetic unless you feel as I do, and
Brecht did:

ON TEACHING WITHOUT PUPILS

Teaching without pupils
Writing without fame
are difficult.

It is good to go out in the morning
With your newly written pages
To the waiting printer, across the buzzing market
Where they sell meat and workmen's tools:
You sell sentences.

The driver has driven fast
He has not breakfasted
Every bend was a risk
In haste he steps through the doorway:
The man he came to fetch
Has already gone.

There speaks the man to whom no one is listening:
He speaks too loud
He repeats himself
He says things that are wrong:
He goes uncorrected.

And so I've tried to get in there, crossing the square with my
mss., on the way to printer, feeling myself a member of the God-

Damned Tribe whether they like it or not—a workman, among others who work.

And have learned to make them hear.

What I make them hear is my poetry. Written entirely without regard to getting them there, you understand.

So I think of this whole letter as a bet between you and me. Am I covered? I remain, Lew Welch

P.S. I'm writing a book called "I Remain," consisting of letters I send to friends. I'd like to include this one, perhaps, but I can't retype it because part of the format is that the letters have to be "real," and try as I may I always tamper, ruin, and finally, maybe, don't even send some dandys. Could you either return this letter, or have someone copy it and send it back? Lew

(If so, also send this P.S., which is part of, as *this* note, too, is.) love, Lew

"The year I was crippled": Welch snapped an Achilles' tendon while playing tennis with Magda Cregg in the summer of 1964. He read Michael Hamburger's translation of Brecht's poem in *The New Statesman* for 24 December 1960; the revised version we give here is from Bertolt Brecht: *Poems 1913-1956* (London: Eyre Methuen, © 1976).

To James Schevill, from 52 Buckelew Street, Marin City,
16 October 1966

Dear Jim, Attached are program notes and a press release for the reading.

I kept trying to make my usual poem line breaks, ending with worthless *****s between paragraphs, so please print as edited. Is more than one page o.k.?

I hope so. Lew

P.S. I have copies which I'll send to [Ralph] Gleason. LW

PRESS RELEASE

Poet Lew Welch, one of the major figures of the new San Francisco Renaissance, appears for The Poetry Center of San Francisco State College on Wednesday, October 26, at The Museum of Art, Van Ness and McAllister Sts., at 8:15 p.m.

Widely published both here and in Europe, Welch is known for the wide range of "voices" in his work, and for a down-to-earth style he sometimes calls "letting America speak for itself."

His many readings have been among those that reshaped the idea of Poetry Reading into its modern form—a new theater art far more flexible, challenging, and entertaining than what we had in the past.

Welch will perform his poems, songs, and plays in a program called "One-Man Plays."

I first read for the Poetry Center in 1959. I said, in the program note: "When I write my only concern is accuracy. I try to write accurately from the poise of mind which lets us see that things are exactly what they seem. I never worry about beauty, if it is accurate there is always beauty. I never worry about form, if it is accurate there is always form."

I phoned that statement from work. I had a dreary, underpaid job for the Bemis Bag factory, and the roar of their presses and bag machinery was almost too loud to think, or talk over.

Since 1959 all kinds of things have happened to me and the world, but I still hold to this statement, absolutely.

What was then the "Beat Generation" is now down to a few survivors, each of whom went his only way. Most of us are gone (as so many makers go early) into prisons, loony bins, penthouses, graves, and the other silences of whatever desperation.

It has been no different for us than for any generation. Witness Rexroth's poem on the death of Dylan Thomas, where he lists the victims he loved, who lost. Then counter this, or any other, with the list of poets, painters, dancers, musicians who lived beyond their fortieth year.

Happily, I'm still alive and am just turned 40. From such a rare height it is possible to say (in defense of my work, and others here or gone), that today, foolish as they may appear to the frightened eye, young America swings much harder than we did, with less fear, and more love.

American poetry, for at least 50 years, has had to screech above the din of a Bemis Bag. Hart Crane's daddy wanted him to manage the family candy factory. Whitman could say it was marvelous to see the muscled workers. But the poets who followed him (who had to be those workers, at jobs) know that there ain't no muscled workers, they's only victims.

Whitman, the roaming spectator, was victimized later. Fancy professors do it, daily, in the state universities. There's a Walt Whitman Savings and Loan in his old home town. It only goes to show what the reward is, if you work real hard and never cheat.

The sound we hear from our tribe is not much different from the thousand sparrows who used to sleep in a palm tree outside my window, once. The racket was unbelievable, but the birds were only arguing about who has the right to sleep, and where.

So, in my poetry, I've tried to keep the din while being accurate to the poise of mind that lets us know what's what. Sometimes I've called this din "Letting America speak for itself." Often it's a depressing job.

But I still have faith that if I do this right, accurately, the sound will emerge a "meaningless din of joy." Because I know that the true sound of living things, a carrot or a tribe, is meaningless, and that we, watching it, feel joy.

This sound, the din of joy, is quite distinct from the sound of the Pentagon, Washington in general and especially Mr. Johnson, the fear-ridden hateful spites of J. Edgar Hoover, and the killing orders of anyone who wants to "boss" anything whether or not the work ought to be done.

Therefore, "One-Man Plays," some of the din of the Tribe, speaking for itself. Accurately.

1967

GROVER SALES: LEW WELCH'S ONE-MAN PLAYS
[From *San Francisco,* January 1967]

Ordinarily, this column does not review poetry readings. I like much contemporary poetry, but not read aloud unless the reader knows what he's doing, like Dylan or e e cummings. Most of the poets I've heard in the Bay Area sound like Parson Weems intoning the Doxology. I've never understood why so many craftsmen who use the tools of meter and timbre seem tone deaf and nonswinging when reading aloud. For boredom that approaches stupefaction, not even bad modern dance can top a dull poetry reading.

It's a mistake to label Lew Welch's recent visitation at the San Francisco Museum of Art a "poetry reading" and thus be dissuaded from attending future performances of this remarkable artist-at-large. Welch subtitles his readings "One-Man Plays," an accurate way of describing a total theatrical experience. In addition to writing powerful and communicative verse, Welch is a musician with a remarkable ear. He composes tunes of disarming simplicity, has a resplendent singing voice well suited to the American ballad styles of Billy Eckstein and Herb Jeffries, both of whom he can imitate with uncanny precision. A superb mimic, his version of Eckstein singing Eliot's *The Waste Land* was one of many delights he held for the Museum audience, which seemed in a justifiable state of whooping hysteria much of the time. It is no exaggeration to say that Lew Welch is funnier by far than many of the comics who played the hungry i. He whistles, chants, improvises, weeps, croons—he is totally involved. Also, he is a very beautiful looking cat, well over six feet, sinewy-thin, with a shock of coppery hair matching the color of his enormous eyeballs.

As a performer, Welch has the extraordinary gift of being "on" with his audience, as authentic and relaxed as in his own living room, and considering he makes public appearances only a few times yearly, such ease of operation is all the more astonishing. Even more unusual, he knows when to get on and get off, something many professionals and practically no poets manage.

Much of Welch's poetry can be viewed as modern sermons, Bob Dylan for mature adults, songs of protest and love that incorporate the sounds, the vulgarisms and the music of our time. Few in the audience will forget the moving, impassioned reading of his "Chicago Poem."

> I lived here nearly 5 years before I could
>   meet the middle western day with anything approaching
> Dignity. It's a place that lets you
>   understand why the Bible is the way it is:
> Proud people cannot live here.

This is not the Chicago of Sandberg but the *Rome* of Juvenal and the *London* of William Blake. "It/ Snuffles on the beach of its Great Lake like a/ blind, red, rhinoceros./ It's already running us down." And the awesome closing:

> You can't fix it. You can't make it go away.
>   I don't know what you're going to do about it.
> But I know what I'm going to do about it. I'm just
>   going to walk away from it. Maybe
> A small part of it will die if I'm not around
>
>   feeding it anymore.

And Welch, who reads his lines with a hypnotic and single-minded intensity, means every mothering word of it.

What should be clear is that an evening with Lew Welch is a far more rewarding experience than most of the so-called "legitimate" entertainment in town and he should not be missed his next time around. If you have teenagers, take them—Welch turns them on! Finally, it is worth mentioning that the Museum audience for Welch's reading included Mr. and Mrs. Jack Morrison; any city that elects a Supervisor who will take his wife to a poetry reading, can't be all bad.

To Jack Shoemaker, from 52 *Buckelew Street, Marin City,*
3 March 1967

Dear Mr. Shoemaker, Yes, I'd be delighted to read in your series.

The terms seem very fair. I'll be driving down & will leave it up to you to figure out what expense that entails.

I would want to read Saturday, April 22. I plan to take Friday off from my job so I can drive leisurely and enjoyably, so I'll arrive Friday evening, or afternoon. Where shall we meet? At your bookstore?

I enclose 3 things:

1) A copy of a recent review of my kind of reading. You may use this in any manner you wish, for publicity, but please see that Grover Sales gets his byline.

2) Four flicks which can be used as tip-ons for posters, newspaper pics, or whatever.

3) A copy of the poem (unpublished) which you can use for your broadside. I am fairly knowledgeable about printing, have studied with Lloyd Reynolds at Reed, and like the clean, traditional style—such as Dave Haselwood uses, for Auerhahn Press. I detest all sans-serif typefaces, for poetry, at least. Good bookfaces, Janson, Caslon, etc. By the way, I think the broadside idea is very good—one of the nice new things about American Poetry.

If all this is ok, please confirm. And thanks for the opportunity. Looking forward (out)   Lew Welch

[Enc. "The Basic Con."]

The Unicorn Bookshop sponsored a series of poetry readings in Isla Vista.

To Lew Welch, from Gary Snyder, Suwa-no-se Island,
3 August 1967

Dear Lew   I'm hardly able to write because where I am is so far from writing or reading—But I thought of you today—and how much at home you'd be here & a boat will be stopping by in a few days & will take mail. 14 people—one year-old boy—on this small island (with 40 village people half a mile away)—an active "Stromboli-type" volcano—coral—we live in thatch houses in a bamboo—banyan—and banana semijungle. The tribe here are/is all artist-Saddhu-wanderers (5 girls) and all workers.

We work a big sweetpotato field—backbreaking clearing out old bamboo roots for planting—

Read by candlelight—gather pine for firewood // fish on the beach—incredibly rich in fish—today I speared undersea a 5-lb beauty with emerald and cobalt specks on an olive and silver ground—with a homemade bamboo spear powered with inner tube // meditate inside a big banyan tree we cleared out // not a car on the island—the boat from Kagoshima stops once a week offshore. The group is going to keep this place (house we are renting—land free to those who'll use it) and a few kids will live here all year.

My girl is here with me and we are going to be married here—on August 6—all the islanders join in later and drink with us her name is Masa Uehara—25—I've known her well over a year. Wish us well. As I wish you and Magda. I hope all goes with you—write (to Kyoto). Love, Gary

To Gary Snyder, from 52 *Buckelew Street, Marin City,*
9 *August* 1967

Dear Gary, What is this I hear you're going to marry some Japanese lady? Good! We've all seen the likes of American broads and I never had a moment's peace till I met my Polish Magda.

Well the revolution is finally happening. Detroit and 40 other cities blew up in July—the 1967 total is 70 cities and towns. Marin City, my home town, blew up a weekend ago so bad we thought it prudent to evacuate ourselves. These niggers are only shooting at Authority: Greyhound buses, cop-cars, fire engines, poverty-program offices. It's not so much a racial revolution as a revolution of the poor. Detroit looting was integrated—spade cats helping white cats into the high window. Not so much about colored skin as about colored TV. TV sets scattered all over Detroit by folks who found them too heavy to get home in all that rifle fire.

I asked a friend of mine (black) if I could join the Black Panthers and help burn it down and he said, "Are you a Panther?" I had to allow as how I wasn't. What a pity! It finally takes off and I can't join, don't want to, can't pass the physical you might say.

And also it's pretty scary living in violence, I really don't want Jeff [Cregg] to get hurt, or Magda, but here is where we live and we just get used to rifle fire (every night for more than two months and the Greyhound bus drivers are quitting the night shift, who can blame them?).

But even more important than that the Meth Freak hippy pushers have got so big the Mafia is moving in and pushers in the Hashbury are getting murdered. Three at least. *And* the acid is untakeable because it may be STP (an Army drug developed to pacify or wipe out the enemy, the trip goes on for 72 hours and 4 of my friends, some of them very strong, are now in loony bins), not to mention the bad shit LSD with Meth in it. Gary, people, good ones, are blowing their minds irreversibly. Like, gone. Away.

Of course there are also the beautiful things. Like George Harrison and his wife appeared in the Hashbury and it was 2 hours before they were recognized. Then George led a huge meaningless parade singing and banging his guitar. He is stone serious about his teacher Ravi Shankar, who, naturally, does not condone drugs. George had purple glasses, in the shape of a heart. His wife is very wild looking. Dumpy, pretty, granny glasses, et al.

Meanwhile, what happened to me was I got hit in the back of my car and got a horrible whiplash. This might be a blessing finally, but right now it really hurts. My eyes are so fucked up I cannot read. But since I have to heal anyway, I figure I'll go to Tassajara and let beautiful little guy straighten my head out. Hot baths too.

I have not been able to kick either tobacco or booze. Shit.

I must tell you about the magic of the mountain we sat on. First, you remember, I found a half pint of Old Crow. Then, yesterday, I returned to the rock and found a ¾ full bottle of beer, and, after sitting there a while, I decided to pick up all litter. Just beside a nasty pile of crap there was a perfectly rolled joint, with incredible power.

I intend to go to Tassajara without cigarettes or booze and do what the man says. I am not strong enough to do it alone.   Lew
[P.S.] Today I got your island-idyll letter. Green with envy. Yam city. I am really sick, but the whiplash will let me take off from work, dry out, stop smoking, and sit with Suzuki in the mtns. and then, later, maybe thousands of $s etc. I have a nice beard now, Magda sends her blessings. Jeff is already famous—I am known as "Jeff's stepfather." Beautiful to have a turned-out son. Try it with your new lady.   All love Gary,   Lew

Tassajara: Zen Mountain Center, Carmel Valley.

To Lew Welch, from Gary Snyder, 31 Nishinoyama-cho,
Shichiku, Kita-ku, Kyoto, 17 September 1967

Dear Lewie—Yes! Got married Aug 6 on Suwa-no-se Island—on
the volcano—my wife's name is Masa ("elegant") and she's very
good and sharp & strong etc.

From here America sounds pretty bad-off. Yet I would be there
to put my (as Allen said) queer shoulder to the wheel of trying at
least to remake or make a new society within the society.

The island was a good job for us. The Japanese kids—no matter
how far out—know how to cooperate and work together. {but then
they're really not very far out.}

SKIN DIVING

This fall is study and zazen 8 a.m. for me. I still drink but I never
did smoke again (except for grass which we have lots of).

Julie Wellings is here—she's in the other room reading the
Hevajra-tantra right now. Masa is cutting up an onion for dinner. I
hope your whiplash hasn't showed bad—that you're better now &
can *read*. (tho it might be good *not* to)   Love to Magda and love
to you.   Gary

1968

To Elspeth Smith, from 52 *Buckelew Street, Marin City,*
6 *January* 1968

Dear Elspeth,   I'm as sorry as you are about the failure to get that
winter class. I had a bad car wreck, whiplash, and haven't been
myself at all. I kept putting off answering you, while drumming up
poets et al., foolish.

I'm all right now, and look forward to the spring class. I can
handle 30 people, so let's put 30 as the limit.

I got such a nice big check. How did you manage that? We've
come a long way in a very few years, thanks to your understanding
and my "savage care," as one of my students put it. (Isn't that
nice?) I'm so touched.

May I get paid for 20 of the 30 on the tutorial thing? My practice
is to have one student before, and one student after, each class.
One hour, each. It makes a long night, but it's worth it to all of us.

Yes, I definitely think we ought to have a poster. The quality,
the kind of people we got last time (as well as the large number),
was largely due to the poster, I'm sure.

· · · · · · · · · ·

AN ENTIRELY DIFFERENT MATTER!
I want to go to Chile. It has been a dream of mine since 1950, but I
haven't been ready until now. Last year, many chance meetings
with people in the Cal.-to-Santiago structure have occurred. Almost
spooky. They all said I was a cinch if I went about it right. But I
wasn't ready, and didn't follow through, and now I don't even have
the right names.

This year I will have a publication of selected works by Grove
Press, and I agreed to it only if I get the Pulitzer Prize. After their
first astonishment they got amused by the idea, and will try it. (You
know it's only a bunch of political bullshit, and they flipped when I
told them it was their turn, and that it might as well go to a good
book as a mediocre one.)

147

Also, now, I can work for almost Chilean wages, having got my affairs, finally, into good shape.

I want a year there, as lecturer or visiting 'Murcan Poet, for myself, my wife and 13 year old boy. I would prefer transportation for the 3 of us, but would settle for transportation for myself. A salary of $5,000 would be groovy, I can settle for less.

Could you help me find the right people to talk to? (I know this isn't your field, but I don't know where to start.)

Could you help me with this? The target should be late 1968 or early 1969, tell them. O.K.?   yours truly,   Lew

P.S. (and this isn't only a put-on), you sure write an accurate letter. I suggest you never take my course. You don't need it. I'm sure you know the other kinds of letters we get. And most of 'em PhDs! Lew

Elspeth Smith was chairperson of the Arts and Humanities program of the University of California Extension during the several years Welch conducted a poetry workshop.

To Sister Mary Norbert Körte, from 52 *Buckelew Street, Marin City,* 12 *July* 1968

Dear Mary,   Thank you for your touching letter, I understand perfectly and am pleased to be used by you as a confidant in this matter or any other. Such decisions are so bleak, alone, they are nearly impossible, or cause unnecessary pain.

I took the liberty to read your letter to Skip [Charles Upton]. He is very proud of your courage—seeing your decision as a truer way of loving Christ, certainly not a cop-out at all.

Still, we both weep in sympathy for what deep agonies must accompany such searchings of the soul. We hold you, and True Belief, so dear. It is all so obvious, why should we suffer so!

Or put it in my natural rage: THOSE CREEPS DON'T DESERVE ONE HOUR OF YOUR TIME, OR ONE RED HAIR ON YOUR HEAD!!! The beauty of your presence makes a mockery of all they say, the beauty of your work mocks all they do.

My new book, *Courses*, has a course in Theology which might help a little:

THEOLOGY

The True Rebel never advertises it,
He prefers His Joy to Missionary Work.

•

Church is Bureaucracy,
no more interesting than any Post Office.

Religion is Revelation:
All the Wonder of all the Planets striking
All your Only Mind.

•

Guard the mysteries!
Constantly Reveal Them!

And just recently I discovered that "Canticle to the Waterbirds"
is a curse—a curse against sea birds, by a man who curses himself.
I checked it out with Skip. He agrees. It's a curse. A curse by a
good man made sick by teachings which call themselves Love!

This business, Mary, is not for the likes of us. Nor was it, when
seen, any business of His. And I mean Jesus.

You and I and Skip and Allen and Gary and Phil and countless
others have taken Orders far more profound than anything Church
can imagine. Even the Orders of Poetry, great as they are, are trivial in the face of the Orders we have taken.

The Poem is not the Poet. The print of the lion on the trail is not
the Lion. In bad moods I see Poetry as the garbage in the wake of
my boat.

Duncan, who talks about the Orders of Poetry, displays, perfectly, the sins of a bad monk. Spicer, taking an even more stern
position on the subject, died at 41. Without heirs.

• • • • • •

Yes! You can now, as always, sit in my living room and hear
even more foolish things than Lenny Bruce. Whoever said you
couldn't? Have you looked at them lately?

Aren't they awful?   Aren't they ugly?

• • • • • •

We are beautiful. We love you. You are welcome.

• • • • • •

Magda just phoned after picketing the trial of Huey Newton. Huey has gained the love of people. Possible tragedy was averted by great love and strong work. That is where you will be now, just as He was. Welcome. We need all the help we can get.

•

I hate to end on a bad note, but I have to. My class didn't fill, so there won't be a reading for you and Phil. Sorry, it was all my own fault. Next time, no blunders.

We keep on spinning the wheel of the Dharma. Sometimes we make mistakes.   No Blame   Lew

To Donald Allen, from 52 *Buckelew Street, Marin City,*
27 *July* 1968

Dear Don,   I want to teach a class at Marin College this fall & in order to do that I need a Credential of Eminence, they call it.

If you truly think I am, indeed, Eminent, please fill in the attached form. Briefly. The job is cinched, this is only formal.

You only have to say one sentence, like, "Lew Welch writes poetry better than anybody else does anything, and, not since Socrates have we had so (such a?) sober and inspiring a teacher."   } or not

Lew Welch

[P.S.] (please do this next week) I enclose form & envelope

1969

To Mrs. Ruth Cole, University of California at Santa Barbara, from 52 Buckelew Street, Marin City, 16 March 1969

Dear Mrs. Cole   Yes, I agree to read on Monday, April 7, at 8:00 p.m. in Isla Vista. With great pleasure. Terms fine etc.
Brief Biog:
    Born Aug. 1926 Phoenix Arizona, sign of Leo. Family lived in many small towns in California. B. A. at Reed College in 1950. Too many years at too many colleges thereafter.
    Have been associated with Beat Generation San Francisco poets since 1957. Live in the mountains and return to S.F., back and forth.
    I read at colleges all over. Teach for U.C. Berkeley Extension. Publish in little mags. Books: *Wobbly Rock, Hermit Poems, On Out, Courses*. At present, preparing mss. for selected works, Grove Press. Translated into Italian, published in Penguin Press British Anthology, & a forthcoming triptych-book with Gary Snyder and Philip Whalen, also Penguin Press. Collected in Grove Press anthology *The New American Poetry, 1945-1960*.
    Who do I meet in Santa Barbara? I'll drive down. Please advise re: accommodations etc. Jack Shoemaker?   yours truly,   Lew Welch

    Penguin Books did publish *The New Writing in the U.S.A.* but did not bring out the "triptych-book."

To Elspeth Smith, from 52 Buckelew Street, Marin City, June 1969

Dear Elspeth,   I'm very sorry to hear that Mr. H doesn't like me because I smell bad, drink gin, and swear, and don't go to Christian churches, and am "*entertainingly* influencing many young people, as well as blacks." (emphasis, mine).

I don't smell bad. I often come to class in my work clothes, since I make my living on the docks and don't have time to go to Marin County to change and then come back to the city. I pride myself on my clean denims. Many people confuse honest, rough clothing with dirty clothing. I am a Ship's Clerk. I don't get dirty because I just stand around and count things and direct the longshoremen at their work.

I do drink, but I am almost never, except at parties, drunk. Many people confuse the rage of poetry (an extremely exhilarated frame of mind, accompanied by an almost supernatural gift of speech—"blarney" if you will) with crazed or artificially induced states. Alas. I have been accused of being crazy or hopped up ever since I was a little boy. Today, I know it frightens people, I try to assuage their fears, but I cannot turn myself off and also teach this daemonic art. Poetry is not for the faint of heart.

I also swear. I have noticed that most people believe in word magic. They believe that the word and the thing are the same. This makes them crazy: they are caught in boxes of word-boxes within word-boxes and can't get out.

Now, strangely enough, the Poet is the only kind of speaker who knows that words are only words. I can call a wheel a monkey wrench, if you want. I don't care. I can say "There never was a Buddha until you came along and I don't like you." I can say all manner of heretical things, because whatever I say, it is, among other things, just blarney. Words.

If, by whatever trick, I manage to jar a person out of his word-boxes, I feel I have done him a favor. I haven't so much taught him anything, as given him an opening into which something new might strike. Something that is not words.

Sometimes I use curses to do this. It is a very old poet/shaman/druid/priest trick. 4,000 years old, at least. People still get frightened by it, but that only proves it still works. If you do this *entertainingly* (I use Mr. H's word, and thank him for his recognition that I am trying to be winning and gentle), great new courage can be instilled in the listener, as I have proved to hundreds of students over the past 5 years of my association with your program. I am sorry that Mr. H got so very frightened. If he had continued the class he might have gotten exhilarated by his new freedom. The rest of the class did. It was a tough class, I admit. But it was also one of my most successful ones. I judge this by the greatly improved work that students gave me (comparing their first efforts, with their later ones), and by the unusually warm thank yous the last night.

I do live in a town which is mostly populated by black people. I do identify with black people warmly, with compassion, even envy (what vigor, what courage, what humor, against what awful odds!). But I do not *incite* my black brothers to violence because I know they will get hurt, decimated, in all likelihood. I do, however, urge them to try to "upset the establishment" because the established order of things is so obviously trying to do them in.

As for the Christ business, Buddha said "If you want to be the Buddha, don't follow me." I think Christ was a fine man. I don't like the way he has been abused by those who claim to revere him, and I think it was partly his fault. He never set his followers free, thereby leaving all manner of loopholes. The Christian cultures have the bloodiest history in the long sad tale of Man. There must be something wrong with that text.

As for the "dope" business, I only said that it is known that poets, seers, artists of all kinds, have made use of the herbs (both fermented and not) of this planet Earth. It is a kind of medicine for the mind. You cannot truthfully recount the history of poetry without mentioning this thing, and I insist upon being a teacher of Truths, not paranoid no-no, hush-hush, nonsense that a change of law would reveal as a lie. The Delphic Oracle lived in a cave and sniffed volcanic gasses. Tennyson put laudanum in his porter. Everybody would rather this weren't true, but I'm sorry, Virginia . . .

Thank you for forwarding a copy of Mr. H's letter to me. Thank you, also, for your understanding of the sometimes almost impossible difficulties of giving an *open* class in poetry, only 10 weeks long.

I have had Physics professors, computer programmers, nurses, doctors, teachers, housewives, whores, thieves, musicians (Joe McDonald of Country Joe and the Fish, for example), transvestites, nuns, the very young and the very old. Some of my students have never even *read* poetry. I welcome them all, and I really do try very hard to give them enough to go by so they can get into this art I love so much.

I wish Mr. H had told me his feelings personally, perhaps we could have come to some better understanding. I am truly sorry I failed him, but that may only mean I am not the right teacher for him. This is often the case. I'm sure if he looks around he'll find some teacher who can help him enjoy his hobby more deeply than he now does. Alas, it appears I am not that man.

Sure. I welcome having "someone check" my class. I teach to share my joy and understanding with all who wish to hear of it. But I cannot do this and, at the same time, pull my punches. If you, or whoever wants to come, will listen carefully to the seemingly rambling way of the dialogue of my class, I'm sure you'll see the punches are ultimately very kind. It's like shaking someone awake on the subway—he might otherwise have missed his stop.

I guess Mr. H woke up grumpy and scared.   yours very truly,

P.S. I have never been in a mental institution. I had a very painful youth, spent nearly 4 years with a psychoanalyst, and worked, by myself, through many nightmares and agonies. I'm far too tough, stubborn, prideful, and smart to ever give in and swoon to a bed in the funny farm. I know things those doctors haven't dreamed of. —Just as Mr. Freud went to the Greek poets, the poets did not come to him.

If it makes anybody feel relieved to believe I am Koo-Koo, let them so think.

P.P.S. I may not have told you that over the past 5 years 3 of my students have come to me with suicidal problems and I have been successful in talking them out of it, by talking them into themselves again. This is always a part of the teaching commitment, as many of my fellow teachers report (I'm talking about real teachers, not parrots of murk).

The majority of my students trust me, sometimes to a degree almost beyond my powers and my strength.

And these few, who are so desperately lost, are the ones I really worry about. They have been lied to so much, they don't even know who they are anymore.

Mr. H certainly knows who he is. I don't worry about him at all. But if I should ever fail one of those others . . .

This draft of a letter was neither completed nor sent.

To Robert D. Wilder, Headmaster, the Urban School of San Francisco, from 52 Buckelew Street, Marin City, 19 June 1969

Dear Mr. Wilder,   I enclose my signed contract, course description, and resume.

Let me congratulate you and your school for the first sane contract I have ever seen. When I taught one semester at College of

Marin I had to fill out a form which had, among others, a question which went "have you ever suffered from undue worry or fear?" They also made me promise I wouldn't burn flags, politicians, draft cards, or money.

I also enclose a ticket to a major public reading to be held on June 30, as per the ticket. I'd be very pleased if you and your friends could come to hear us. The cause is righteous. Further, you might want to see, in action, what kind of nut you have hired.

I can't tell you how delighted I am to join your school. Until, hopefully, June 30th   Lew Welch

COURSE DESCRIPTION
Creative Writing   Instructor: Lew Welch

The nature and usage of American English will be studied with especial emphasis on daily speech, the source language we use on our streets and in our homes. The best writing has always been written in this living tongue, it has never come from libraries, dictionaries, grammar books and the like, for these last are long after the fact. While examples from great American writers will be studied, the art of listening to contemporary speech and then using it will be the heart of the course. Call it ear training.

Grammar and usage will be looked at in the modern manner of structural linguistics—a lively new approach to the real problem of verbal communication, not just a bunch of rules. The history of our language will be studied to show how languages constantly change in uncontrollable, almost organic, ways.

Creative writing is seen as the art of transforming thoughts and observations into words. Poetry, Plays, Novels, Songs, Essays, all will be called "Writing." The student is encouraged to find his own range of writing, he will not be bogged down by arguments about genre, style, existing forms, rules and so forth. You cannot analyze writing until that kind of writing has been written.

Frequent field trips will be taken into the City's parks, bus stations, and streets, where the students will practice observing as writers do, and listening as writers listen. From these notes and visions will come the stuff of written exercises.

The Instructor
Lew Welch is one of the strongest of the poets identified with the "Beat Generation" of the early 1950s. His popularity has spanned 2 generations at least, and he now speaks both to the new

generation of young, active students, and to the older academic world of liberal scholars and professors.

He has published 4 books and appears in countless journals of the avant-garde "little magazine" world. In spring of 1970 his first major collection, *Ring of Bone, Poems 1950 to 1970* will appear from Grove Press. He appears in many textbooks and anthologies of modern verse here and in Britain, and has been translated into Italian and Spanish.

He is noted for powerful performances of his work, standing high among those who have recently established the art of Poetry Reading as perhaps the most exciting verbal theater in America today.

A graduate of Reed College in 1950, he studied more than 3 years in the graduate school of the University of Chicago, majoring in structural linguistics, philosophy, and history.

He teaches the Poetry Workshop for the University of California Extension, a position he has held for 5 years, and is the frequent guest lecturer and visiting Poet at special university programs all over the United States and Canada.

To Philip Whalen, from 52 *Buckelew Street, Marin City,*
25 *June* 1969

Dear Philip,   Just because I write you so seldom doesn't mean anything except I stay lazy and inefficient. We all miss you. I wrote a review of *On Bear's Head* for the *Chronicle* of June 22nd. Do you want a copy? I suppose you got the screams of dismay, anguish, fury, caused by $17.50 *the* copy—all attempts to express the universal love we have for you here & the really sinister way the dying Mind of 'Murca is trying to pack its trunk with *everything* so as not to be lonely in whatever Bardo. General hysteria so freaky now it's not even (somehow) frightening. Nobody ever tried to make money off poetry before & we marched beneath machine guns on Berkeley roofs attempting to say it's wrong to kill folks for making a park & then fucking in it. Best shot of the Berkeley March was a lady whose house was on the route passing out free *Pernod*! from a giant washtub—and in John Muir Sierra cups yet! Several cases @ $8.50 *the* bottle!

I had my most beautiful death yet, a 3-month puss-bomb which popped about June 1 and blew me A (hyphen) WAY. I was escorted

by Milarepa and Tamalpais on wings of Turkey Buzzard which, by
the way, I find I ride. (How desperately I wanted to ride Cougar.)
Learned how to kill demons. Don't *ever* drink booze now, don't
like it, drank my fill. Will forward death notes & demon-battle
soon. Fascinating. All this energy: Got all poems together and in
Don's hands for Grove book *Ring of Bone* (250 pp) next spring.
New Book *Song Mt. Tamalpais Sings* all but finished. Start of new
American religion. Mind of Don Juan, Ishi, Peyote, etc. is, I discover, what the Asian Mind would have been if Asia had not got
crowded. No sloppy Injun veneration, dig, but Tamalpais singing it
to *me*. We are what our land and air is, etc. Poems really lovely not
writ by me at all. Thank goodness I practiced. Everything going
just right at last, not even ecstatic. Better. All warnings about that
now understood. I eat food now.

— — — — — — * — — — — — —

All Praises, Tamalpais,
Perfect in Wisdom & Beauty
She of the Wheeling Birds

Lew

To Lew Welch, from Philip Whalen, c/o Education Dept.,
YMCA, Sanjo-Yanaginobamba, Nakagyo-ku, Kyoto, 3 July 1969

Dear Lewy,   D. R. Carpenter mailed me a copy of your *Chronicle*
review. I feel enormously flattered & pleased & delighted & at the
same time wish that the book amounted to something—& after
all, it just *don't*, not really. Any one of your poems is more authentic & solid than this whole wretched book.
   I wander & teach & meditate & wrestle with Bach on an out-of-
tune electronical "organ" & dream of a solitary elegant forest/
seashore life in Oregon . . . while getting endless metaphysical vita-
mins pumped into me by Kyoto & environs. It is really cuckoo to
live in a scene which has once been the setting of several REAL
works of art, real spirit breakthroughs, *real* violence of ambition,
war, grope, grab, konk, slice chop—this town has been burnt &
pounded level two or three times in the last 1000 years & keeps
coming on in spite of everything, as THE CAPITAL—even though
the taste is now not even false taste but a kind of revolting prudery

157

& "propriety" 900 times worse than Dickensian London &c.—
Something here survives all this, I say, & zaps me inexpressibly. A
reality, an authenticity I demand & now am *having*—how to tell
you *that* . . .   Love to Magda & to you.   Phil

Welch reviewed Whalen's *On Bear's Head* in the *San Francisco Chronicle*, 22
June 1969; it is reprinted in *How I Work as a Poet*.

To Terence Cuddy, from 52 *Buckelew Street, Marin City,*
1 *September* 1969

Dear Terry,   It sure was fun to read at your house. Richard and I
both feel it was one of the warmest and |most| intelligent audiences
we've ever had. Please tell your friends how good they made us
feel. Harold Dodd wrote a touching thank-you note that also
helped get me through a bad day.

This has been a hard summer for me. Bad depressions and big
changes I don't seem to be able to handle very well. I just had my
43rd birthday and feel old and feeble, somehow. Mostly it's a
matter of stopping the booze absolutely—I don't really drink
enough to matter but even that little is ruining my health and
frame of mind. It's almost like being allergic to the stuff. Well, I'm
into my fifth try at going dry. A drag.

I'm working on a funny little song I want to lay on you. Maybe
you can find a good country tune for it.

THE TRAILER IS LEAKY

1.
The trailer is leaky
I lost all my teeth

My old man just left me
My boy friend is broke

The baby's got colic
I've got poison oak

Fox in the henhouse

2.

The puppies are blind
The dog's throwing up

The toilet is plugged
and the kitten has ringworm

Mother is on the
five-thirty bus

Fox in the henhouse

And there ought to be a way to work in Richard's beautiful line:
"Two-timing women, 5-day drunks, and cars with bad transmis-
sions." The darned little lyric always makes me laugh, and I
thought maybe you and the boys might get a kick out of remembering the dumb Oakie troubles that torment us all out here in the
cruel world. You could no doubt think of other verses. And it
might get your mind off your troubles inside the bars.

How does it look about getting out? I think I could help you get
some work down at the docks if you can get out before Xmas.
Work is pretty good usually until Jan. 1st, and I'm almost sure I
could get the dispatcher to realize your predicament. You make
$35 a day @ 4.88 an hour. In winter the work falls off, but you
could get a good start before Xmas. (Maybe make enough to buy
your car with a bad transmission.)

There's a really fine new book out by Gary Snyder. *Earth House
Hold.* It's most of his essays. A truly religious book of startling
brilliance. No dirty words or anything, I'm sure the Chaplain would
want it in his library. Probably the most important book of essays
written by people roughly our own age. It's a New Directions book
at $5, available through City Lights.

Have the boys been reading the books I laid on them? I hope so.

The dogger and Magda send their love. I'll try to find time to
come by and see you. I start teaching 2 classes in September, one
of them to high-school freshmen. I look forward to it—it might just
snap me out of my downer.   good luck old buddy   Lew

"your house": San Quentin, where Welch and Richard Brautigan read from their
work on 22 August 1969.

159

Dear Sir, I've learned that Mr. T. Cuddy, A-53192-A, is being considered for parole, and that any help from his friends will help his cause. I couldn't be happier than to have a chance to help Terry. He is like a brother to me. Further, he is a brother in the Arts.

I am a poet, scholar, and teacher. Recently Richard Brautigan and I read our poems and talked to a most appreciative audience at San Quentin (see *San Quentin News,* 22 August 1969). It was Terry's energy that caused this event to happen.

As a poet and teacher I have seen, known, and taught many people of every kind. You might say that I, in a modest way, am an expert on human behavior and value—that has been my lifetime work.

Rarely have I known a more gifted, loving, outgoing and gentle man as Terry. He has traveled a hard road. On it he has sometimes stumbled. But he could not, knowingly, hurt a soul if he tried.

Most of his "crimes" were those of youthful ignorance; the latest was surely one born out of fear and foolishness. He is older now, has suffered the consequences, and far more sure of himself and his value to others.

When I visited Terry he was very sorry and ashamed about his foolish escapade that put him back "in." He really doesn't want that to happen again. He wants out, and wants to stay out.

Cuddy is one of the finest poet-singers in America. He was just on the verge of being recognized, in a big way, as such. He is needed out here. There is much trouble in this world that a fine poet-singer-actor can ease. Please give him the chance to help us all.

To keep a man of such gifts confined in jail is a shame. We need him out here. We will, and he has many friends, do everything we can to befriend this outstanding man. yours, hopefully, Lew Welch

*To Lew Welch, from Philip Whalen, Fukuoji-cho 82, Utano,
Ukyo-ku, Kyoto, 30 September 1969*

Dear Lewy,   I just got a note from Gary, with a snapshot of Masa
& Kai & himself all in a row among the trees & grasses. He says
you are all nervous again, so I thought I'd write to you immediately
to say: SHAKE NOT, NEITHER SHALT THOU SHUDDER NOR TREMBLE
QUIVER THROB NOR THRONG, for LO! the world & the Flesh & the
Devil ain't worth it, Selah! For the world itself trembled here 3 or 4
minutes on end, shaking me & my little house & the hand-hewn
bamboo chandeliers & candleabra {CANDELABRA!} swayed like
coco palms in a ravening wind—yet it was only temporary. My
stash was safe. And there is a grand shewing of Paul Grogan's
painting here now, & Sandor Burstein arrives tomorrow & I shall
conduct him into the presence of exquisite beauties & magnifi-
cences, the 20 minutes or so he plans to be in Kyoto. Have you
considered the Advantages of a sea voyage? I doubt that it would
hurt you & Magda any at all to take a slow boat out of San
Francisco, to land at Kobe where I could meet you & bear you all
away to Kyoto for a while. Make Albert come too. Tell the long
shore union it's a medicable necessity & you {& they} can take it
off their {your} several income taxes. Or try Europe or {at long
last} Peru. Traveling is, in itself, so occupying & maddening &
exciting that it gives one a whole new view of the general self—
at least for a while. "Look at all that beauty out there—the sails of
the herring fleet." {S. Beckett} and I would love to see you &
Magda, & I bet Magda would wig out with all the colors & trees &
flowers & gardens. Please try to get better. We all still love you.
Love to Maria.   Phil

Maria: Magda Cregg's German shepherd.

*To Philip Whalen, from 52 Buckelew Street, Marin City,
14 October 1969*

Dear Philip,   Thanks for your concern and your invitation, I'm
taking care of the first and I think I *will* try to visit you next spring.
Is May a good month? You speak. I'll try to talk Albert into going
along, too.
    I guess I finally really hit bottom on the alky trip (a bummer

from in front)—ended up in the hospital malnourished and flipped out, body screaming for peace and mind on bad death/suicide trips for the first time in my life. Am three weeks dry now & have every hope I'm really off the sauce at last. Had two glasses wine at lunch the other day & got instantly muddleheaded & had all-afternoon headache. I don't like that mind anymore, but the sober one is hard to get used to: "finding yourself suddenly in a world which requires itself to be taken seriously." (Cocteau) I realize I've led a life constantly in a state (either natural or induced) of overexcitement. Must learn this new peace (often misread by me as torpor).

All my poems now at Grove for *Ring of Bone, Poems 1950–1970*. Maybe out by spring. New poems coming out of present mind with peyote-grass help for visions and/or actual writing.

Have 2 teaching jobs now—get "A" book Union Thursday—get a settlement on car-wreck 2½ years ago—Magda still puts up with me, quite cheerfully considering all. So, money, fame, peace, all mine if I only give in. It terrifies me! Dick Baker says you're even fatter than *that*! Magda sends love—me too!   Lew

[P.S.] Also, Skip Upton (my only heir) gets full-page reviews, windows in City Lights, and is learning to write more economically. In my high-school class is a 17 year old girl who writes as spooky as a Bronte. Perfect sense of sentence and paragraph, but spells British and dotes on the subjunctive (too slow!). Spare. Frederica Carlblom for the record. Perhaps I can save her some time.

Gary has never been more relaxed and warm. That son of his better than an *inka*. Masa w/big belly and smile fears Joanne. Sufi Sam Lewis is a student in my U.C. class—strange enlightened little man. I watch the last pelicans every chance I get. How's June in Japan?   love   Lew

To Lew Welch, from Philip Whalen, Fukuoji-cho 82, Utano, Ukyo-ku, Kyoto, 5 November 1969

Dear Lew, I'm breaking in a new Osmiroid pen point. {SKRAATCH!} June in Japan is hot, & the monsoon runs from about the middle of June through to the middle of July. May has the big historical Aoi Matsuri which Lady Murasaki & others have written about. July has stupendous Gion Matsuri, which is great but the weather then is boiling & steaming. The latter part of September is good, & in October lots of paintings & statues & places which are shut up all the rest of the year can be visited & seen. April is gorgeous, the cherry blossoms all are real & the weather is great. Actually, April May & ½ June are quite nice—½ September, all October & ¼ November are splendid. The first ½ of September is still hot & sultry. The middle ¾ of November, on through to April 1 are too fucking C O L D, just as the last part of June until mid-September boils & sizzles & steams & fries & BUGS. You will be welcome whatever the season. I'm glad to hear that your book is all set to come out—but dealing with the N.Y. book publishing business is sure a drag. I'm worrying now about typing a ms. to give to Don Allen for Four Seasons Press, he wants 50 pages, & I still haven't started the machine &c. But any day now. In the meantime, I do a little here & there in current notebooks—but nothing really exciting. I wish I were doing a nice delightful & edifying novel. Having Kerouac die just now is upsetting. It reminds me that I don't have all the time in the world in which to finally get around to writing something considerably better than I've been able to do so far. Give my love to Magda & Maria. Take good care of yourself. Write soon. Phil

1970

To Elizabeth Richardson, from 52 *Buckelew Street, Marin City,* 18 *January* 1970

Dear Mrs. Richardson,   This is to confirm our telephone conversation of a few weeks ago. I am to be resident poet at Colorado State College from June 15 to July 20, 5 weeks, for $3,000, a position I eagerly look forward to. You asked that I forward some of my books, which you will find, enclosed.

Alas, I can't send 2 copies of *Hermit Poems* as you requested, because there are only 5 left in the whole world. I enclose one.

I have delayed this letter waiting for my newest book *The Song Mt. Tamalpais Sings*, to come from the printer, but Gary Snyder phoned last night telling me you had requested a book list from him (about me) and I'm going to the mountains to ski today and I got the impression from Gary that you'd like books and information right away. So I'll send that book (2 copies) within the week, but not right now.

I enclose a copy of a review of one of my major poetry readings to give you an idea of how I work. I believe the Poet is also Singer, Actor, and (hopefully, if the Prince would only listen) Advisor to the Prince. I think Grover Sales' review of that evening is about right as a description of the Poet-as-performer as I enact it.

• • •

My teaching is very personal and elastic. I let the people in the class determine the form of the class—you might call it the Socratic or (I prefer) the "counterpunch" technique. I try to find out what the real questions of the actual students are, and then build a dialogue out of that. I don't hammer home doctrines.

But I insist on real care from the students, and a sweeping survey of *all* writing (suggesting to each student which books *he*, personally, will find especially valuable, so there is no basic text-list, but I usually hit at 50 books or more in a course of this length).

Because of my education at Reed and at University of Chicago I hold to the historical approach to learning, but unlike those systems I like to *start from the present and go back*. If you start with Homer you seldom get further than Donne. If you start with Ginsberg (or, better, with what was read by whatever poet at the coffee gallery last night) and *go back*, you get to Homer quite easily, and you get the Persians and Chinese and Chaucer and the Romans quite naturally and organically.

My system seems easier than the forward-history notion, but it gets the student into more work, quicker. They really get a terrible bibliography to read—one which, in the case of good students, might take 20 years to cover. A lifetime, for me.

I do it this way because I learned this way. I started with W.C. Williams and Gertrude Stein and Kenneth Patchen, and I worked back to our fathers. With, I say praising them, great joy. Great joy!

The position of my teaching is (1) Writing is a fine thing to do, and (2) Not to know the work of 4,000 years of good men killing themselves to say it honestly is *sinful*! So read a lot if you want to write. Those people save us a lot of time. That's why we call them "immortal."

But I do not intimidate! I think a good teacher should give a student a great writer, Whitman let's say, as naturally as one introduces an acquaintance to a notable friend. Perhaps they will become friends, too. It is up to the student. Whitman is always available.

We read student work from a position of this nature, we do not offer a course where people take ego-trips about their own precious little verses. We are discussing and producing poetry.

· · ·

My family includes: me, my wife Magda, my son Jeff 15 yrs, my dog (a big, male, German shepherd of sweet disposition). We prefer to live simply, in the country, but maybe it would be better to have a house where students could visit at all hours.

I intend to spend a lot of time trout fishing and hiking.

Is 2 hours a day about right for the teaching part?

And I will perform my own works at least once (an evening such as Sales describes), and will be more than available to all.   yours truly,   Lew Welch

"Happy Birthday Poem" for Richard Brautigan, 30 January 1970

JANUARY 30, 1970

Dear Richard,

On this very day, in 1889, Franklin
Delano Roosevelt was born. Had he lived,
he would now be 81 years old.

Would he have liked your books?

What present would he give you on
this mutual birthday?

A chest of California grapes?

Lew

To Katharine George, from 52 *Buckelew Street, Marin City,*
15 *February* 1970

Dear Katharine,   It was such a treat to get your yearly newsletter.
It got me all messed up in my head about whether or not I'd rather
be there where you guys are, or here where I am. I really feel
closer to you and your crazy boys than I do to any family, either
my own or any others, around here. The world, as it is known in
this area, even, is really going down hill fast.

Not that I have any complaints, personally. There is a lot of easy
money coming my way, Magda and I are perfectly happy, the
house is comfortable and placed in a way where we don't feel at all
crowded & no one can build around us to shut off the view (please
feel free to fall by here any time, and for however many days or
weeks, if you need shelter down this way, we have more than
enough cheap room & it's handy to the City), but still we wonder
what we're doing in this madhouse of a Bay Area. I'm sure (have
checked it out) that the Bay Area is better than any urban area in
the world, but it just may not be good enough for those, like us,
who are blessed with the choice of moving away as a real possibility. I am still not bought.

This coming year (I'm going to make this a newsletter from the
Welchs, looking forward) I have finally got into the big deals, such

as they are, of the world of Poetry. In March I go to [Vancouver] Canada for $400 for one day, in May I go to Salt Lake City, Pocatello, and Logan, for $200 a stop, in June I go to the big one, Greeley Colo., as resident poet for $3,000 for only 5 weeks, my big book (all my work since 1950) coming out in about June or July with a $1,000 advance and whatever royalties later, and I have two good teaching jobs that add up to nearly $200 a month, so it all adds up to the fact that I'll make over $6,000 this year *as a poet*!

All it means, really, is that after working free for 25 years the bastards are finally paying me.

But it is a real relief after all the struggling and especially sweet to know I got where I wanted to get *on my own terms*, not one single conscious act of cheating or letting another cheat me. So that now every one of the above jobs is a job I would rather do than not do. It is like getting paid for what you only want to do anyway.

And notice the locations! All the big Western States I love so much. Huge hiking, fishing, and exploring missions with Magda, all on an expense account!

I really worried about you when all those ferocious rains came down, so was much relieved that it wasn't nearly so bad as the '64 business. And your Sommes Bar job sounds perfect.

We were so happy to be in a position to help a little with Tom and Cindy's problem. Tell Tom he's got a real good wife there, so pretty and so smart. Of course, that's the least he should expect (just like me), but then it doesn't always work out that way.

We must have got our wires crossed on the "story about Sam" business, I never wrote one. I wanted to write a story about how we all buried Hoopie's first baby, and about how Sam showed up on a fire so drunk he couldn't walk & cried about how this all used to be his happy hunting ground, and there he was a drunk, blue-eyed Swede to all appearances, but I never got around to it. Maybe you could lock me in a cabin up there and give me food, booze, and occasional visits by young ladies, and not let me out until I wrote all that down, then I'd do it.

But I did write a book, a small one, about my stay at Salmon River. One night Dave invited me to dinner (or I should say I stayed so long one evening he and Marge *had* to invite me) and Dave read Robert Service poems to me and I read some of my Salmon River Poems (*Hermit Poems*) and we got very drunk and weepy, and when I read him the one about "The Lady in the Sky," Dave said, "Why that's the moon!"

167

I don't think I gave you one of those books, there are only 4 left in the whole world and you could get $50 for it if you were bad enough a bitch to sell it, but I know you aren't quite that bad, so I enclose one. The handwriting is mine.

*

Jack Boyce is really a successful person. We see each other almost every week. He's building a beautiful house of 16 × 16 heartwood redwood beams he got from an old railway trestle. It's huge. But he and his wife are split up now, childless, and he's going to change his way again. I hope he gets to stop by and see you as he wants to.

*

I know what you mean about "some of them are very nice," re the hippies at Black Bear. Richard Marley is a very good cat and I'd trust him like a brother, but I don't see how he can bear some of the folks that hang out there from time to time. Of course, I have all of this long distance, so I'm not naming names.

It all comes down to the same thing. Just because you're "hip" doesn't mean anything at all. We're all just people. I bet you know some Indians who aren't welcome in your house. Let's keep taking it one by one, person by person, or we all get very wrongheaded.

*

Accepting anyone *because of* his race or style, is as bad as *rejecting* someone because of his race or style. I insist that this short life of ours is far more precious than either, and that we must know each other face to face or not at all.

*

I also enclose a copy of my newest book, *The Song Mt. Tamalpais Sings*. I think I'm getting close to the real voice, the mind, that those of us, like you and me, who are White Indians, have.

Some of us really love this land, in the way the Amerindian knew and loved it. I'm not ashamed that I'm not Indian (how foolish, I can't change that), but I know, also, I am not a member of the rapers who came upon this piece of Earth and treated it so ruthlessly.

My teacher is this gentle mountain I live on. Ask Tom about how beautiful she is. She rules the Bay Area, and I am now her chief poet. It is only for this that I stay.

*

Perhaps we'll be dropping by this summer, after the long tours of Colorado, Idaho, and Utah. Maybe August.

I think of you all, often.   with love   Lew

To Robert D. Wilder, from 52 Buckelew Street, Marin City,
13 May 1970

Dear Bob,   After long consideration I regret to say I must discontinue my class at Urban School for the remainder of this school year.

The present crisis, crises, of our nation have made it impossible for me to teach a class in writing. My heart and mind are simply not with it. And though I could reconstruct my class to be a discussion of our frightening situation, I feel that others more qualified than I should do this. My students are all very much aware of my position regarding the war and the issues of civil rights opportunities. It would avail little to keep repeating myself.

I am now taking so much time off from my work, I don't feel able to take yet another day off to reach so few. I must husband my energies and attempt to make what small influence I do have effective on as broad a scope as possible.

I am painfully aware that this position is an admission of defeat. I admit that my voice has been silenced, temporarily, by those I call my enemies, for silencing the normal, life-loving teachers is precisely what the fascistic mind wants.

I believe that teaching should be done in small groups, but the situation demands of me that I seek larger audiences with every hour I can spare. It is time to drop the plowshare and pick up . . . what? I don't really know.

Perhaps if enough of us act hard enough, especially in the next month, this ghastly business can be stopped. I think that time is running very short, indeed.

Thank you for the opportunity to work for Urban School. It was an experience I'll always remember with fondness. Naturally, you may deduct my pay for the classes I shall not teach, if you so wish.

Thanking you and the kids, I remain   Lew Welch

To David Meltzer, from Greeley, Colorado, 12 *June* 1970

Dear David,   I am typing this on an Olympic typewriter I rented
in Greeley, Colorado. We also rented a small apartment that is in a
perfect Norman building on a campus of elms and large lawns. The
wind brings tides of the scent of bullshit from the Greeley feeding
pens, the largest feeding pens in the world, even the steers from
Olema are fattened here. The by-product is horrific. It grows faster
than the meat and is harder to sell. I figure this is a perfect place
for a bullshit artist, a slinger.

Visited Jim Koller and Drum Hadley in Santa Fe. Very impressed
by that little city—the only place I've seen outside the bay area
where I could conceivably live. A vast peace from the land and
sky, and perfect adobe houses placed so you never feel your neigh-
bors. The whole town is one-story high and the trees are a little
higher than that. Indians in the square with real jewelry. I was so
overwhelmed to see something one might really want to buy that I
couldn't part with a nickel.

Gregory Corso and I rapped 2 nights running about everything.
He is in fine shape right now, but he sure takes up a lot of room and
I fear he has run out of places to stay. Frumkin is hoping to get him
on the staff at Albuquerque next year. Gregory feels "out on a
limb," but he's clean of drugs and very cheerful and brilliant.

I don't have any photographs except the rather blurry ones Jim
Hatch took years ago and which we used in *On Out* (there are
other, very similar poses). I don't think Jim has the negatives at this
time. There are also those flicks by Fred McDarrah used in *The
Beat Scene* which are very flattering but, again, from a long time
ago, circa 1960. It's been a real drag for years. People take my picture all the time but never get them in focus or catch me weird or
it's all dark and you can't possibly reproduce them.

Maybe, if you're in a hurry, you'll want to go to my place and dig
out the glossies taken by Jim Hatch. They are in my file cabinet,
toward the back of the, I believe, top drawer in a manila folder
labeled "flicks." Maybe you could get something out of them.
Terry Cuddy is living there now and you could phone him and feel
free to poke around my files. I won't be home until nearly
September.

Also, I'll see if they've got a photographer here in Greeley, at the
school.

While getting my stuff together for this trip I came across the, some of them anyway, original versions of "Spring Rain Revolution at the Forks." I'm going to try to disinter that poem in the next 5 weeks—a fascinating poetry problem. I think I can now hold it back *there, then.* [Lew]

David Meltzer wanted photos for *The San Francisco Poets*, which he was editing. "Spring Rain Revolution at the Forks" became "Preface to Hermit Poems, The Bath" and "He Greets, Again, the Open Road."

To Clifford Burke, from Department of English, University of North Colorado, Greeley, 13 June 1970

Dear Clifford,   I feel so bad about the Eliot incident I don't know how to express myself. You were right to be angry. Of course I have every right not to like Eliot, to see him as a formidable foe, but I don't have the right to talk to my students, who have an unfortunate tendency to adore my presence and not to challenge my thoughts or prejudices, I have no right to speak to these people as facetiously and crookedly as I was that night. It is against truth and poetry and I am sorry and will never do it again.

But even worse than that I can't bear to think the Eliot incident will make you think less of me to the extent you won't feel as enthusiastic about our printing venture as we were feeling earlier that night. I really need your skills and understanding, without them my poetry will continue to be unavailable and I dread the way most big printers will butcher the lines. I didn't know, didn't think, I had the right to choose my printer, it never occurred to me in my egocentricity, or I would have bound Grove to have you, in my home town, do the printing. I shall, with your permission, always so order in the future. I really think you are the best printer/poet in America, better even to my eye than Haselwood at his peak, though he was brilliant, but there was something too spaced too blocky for the perfect job unless he was printing McClure.

I think we can proceed with almost certainty on the assumption that Grove will not print *Ring of Bone* at all. They will dally, and when the date runs out will try for an extension, and I won't give it to them. My contract has it that the book must come out on or before Jan. 30, 1972. Between now and that date I think we can print most all of it, ourselves, handsomely and right, and then can have whatever new publisher (I am thinking about getting Richard

171

[Brautigan]'s Sterling Lord lady to be an agent) have you as the printer and book designer.

This way we'll have most of the hard work done before the big book is tackled—all proofread and read again after it is on the street—and the real *Ring of Bone* collection will be beautiful beyond all believing. It is really the only important thing (*thing*) I have to be doing now and if, alas, as it appears, it's going to take 2 years, super right for a change. See *On Bear's Head* for example. The sad result of expediencyitis.

The University of Northern Colorado at Greeley is a beautiful campus with 80-foot elms and lots of grass and buildings either pseudo Norman or Victorian, very red, brick. They put me up in a professor pad in one of the Norman buildings only a hundred yards from where I teach. The gardens are positively English. Peonies and columbine. Tennis courts everywhere. I have a garage for the truck. Very plush.

Tomorrow night, Sunday, I read for the Centennial at Greeley, and tonight I go to dinner at Dr. Neal Cross' place—he being a fine gentleman who is sort of my sponsor. He wrote a textbook on Humanities which is now taking off, I think I remember seeing it.

But Greeley itself is something else. The feeding pens are just as they say. Bullshit smells all day and night. No bars. You go out of the city limits and drink in miserable Oakie bars or plastic motels.

There is not one black person in Greeley. I have yet to see an Indian. There are no Mexicans. There are no winos and there is no skid row. The cows are fat.

Today we went to Cheyenne Wyo. and bought $100 worth of western clothes. I finally found my hat. It cost only $3.75. It gives me a headache but I'm going to wear it till it doesn't.

I bought Magda a pair of Tony Lama boots. She looks beautiful in them and sends her love.   later   Lew

"the Eliot incident": Welch had told Burke that he had run down T. S. Eliot in a class discussion and Burke called him on it. Sterling Lord: a literary agent in New York City.

172

SEVEN POSTCARDS TO RICHARD BRAUTIGAN

From Greeley, CO, 3 June 1970

Dear Richard,   Here we are in Greeley looking at TV in a motel. Greeley has no booze inside city limits. There are big trees here. Elms.   Lew & Magda

From Greeley, CO, 13 June 1970

Today we went up to Cheyenne and bought $100.00 worth of good Western clothes. I have, at last, my first hat. It gives me a headache. Right now I like Greeley.   Lew

From Rock Springs, WY, 20 July 1970

We are now in Rock Springs, Wyo. where the talk is about a hippy who ate the heart of a man he killed.   Lew

From Livingston, MT, 21 July 1970

After teaching for 5 weeks I dreamed all night about new classes and am, presently, a real wreck despite Yellowstone & Tetons. Lew

From The Dalles, OR, 23 July 1970

Today we found a live owl impaled on barbed wire in Idaho. I set him as free as his slim chance was.   Lew
(Title—Lost Pet)

From Willow Creek, CA, 7 August 1970

When I was in Woodland Washington I got badly bitten on the right thumb by an old lady sheep.   Lew

From Willow Creek, CA, 7 August 1970

Dear Richard, How were things in London? Things in the big West were.   Lew

To Jack Shoemaker, from 52 Buckelew Street, Marin City,
23 September 1970

Dear Jack,   Here are copies of the Riddles, and photocopies of the drawing. Magda had them do the copies negative and positive to give a night and day effect—and/or—the idea being you could have the back cover day (or night) and the front the other. (You could split it down the middle with an eighth-inch white space to give room for the register of the spine.) And it occurred to me we could *print* the title in rectangle, rather than tip it on, with almost the same effect.

Of course we could also go just one way with the front and back both the same.

As I said, I'm very anxious to get this started. Right now I only have *Courses* in print, as you know.

Let's get together soon as we said   Lew

Jack Shoemaker's Sand Dollar Press was preparing to bring out a second edition of *The Song Mt. Tamalpais Sings* with Magda's drawing on the cover.

To Lew Welch, from Gary Snyder, Kitkitdizze,
Nevada County, CA, 21 *December* 1970

Thurs. night
Lew— I got your little shovel. It still keeps snowing and then melting, we still need chains. Still looks like January for us tho a lot depends on my mother's (hospital) condition.[. . .]

(about the land next to us) The Realtor handling it is "Ebb" Pounds, of Sacramento. He wants too much. But John thinks if people go to him with a solid proposal and hold to it, he'll come way down.

Sun night
—Snow's stuck, and started snowing again—it's @ 10″ now. Went out this morning OK, but if it keeps up we'll get stuck   Ho Ho

We think definitely January for visit—probably 8-9-10 Jan. (And I'll be down again Jan 29 for benefit Reading for Tarthang Tulku.) Resist Christmas and sail into the New Year!   Love,   Gary
P.S. Armed peasants willing to die are the match for any "state"

1971

Dear Jim,   Glad to hear *Coyote* is alive again. I enclose a poem,
my new book, and a sample of the kind of thing being faced here in
the Bay Area.

The riddles in the book are real riddles, with answers. I can't get
anyone to believe this unless I keep insisting. Only one person so
far has solved bowing and clasping hands. Soon I hope to have a
buzzard feather to send anyone who solves those two correctly,
which feather gives the person the right to verify the correct
answer from others. There really is only one right answer to
bowing, and only one right answer to the riddle of hands. They are
the first American koans. Solving them gives a deep spiritual
insight. They aren't easy, it took me 3½ years to solve the riddle of
hands & I invented the question. Or discovered it.

So, even though they've been printed in this book I'd like to see
them in *Coyote.* They are certainly the most Shamanistic poems
I've ever written. People really get hooked by them once they
realize they are true riddles, not just pomes. 4 guys in San Quentin
are going dingy trying to solve them. They aren't even close. One
guy at Reed almost has bowing. (Bowing, by the way, is easier than
Hands.) The commentaries by the Red Monk should be read
carefully. They are helpful.

If you do publish the riddles maybe you should also print the
above [¶ 2] so people can get into them. People just won't *believe*
poetry. Cocteau: "The poet doesn't desire to be understood, he
wants to be *believed.*" [. . .]

· · · · · · · · · · ·

"The simple smiling face of survivors." Here there is the panic of
those who finally realize it's all over, that all that ecology stuff was
true, that soon there won't be anything but chickens & they all
horrible albino-freaks. Even Bill Brown quit drinking.

175

Huge pleas for Gary and me to come to Bolinas to help with decisions. We'll go.

Keith L[ampe] really freaking out. Birds in everybody's back yard. Pecked children.

Quite likely every lagoon and marsh in the Bay Area will be sterile forever.

And so forth.

. . . .

Magda and I are breaking up. I'm going to build a cabin at Gary's plot. Ginsberg gave me rights to his land, free. Allen is too much. (You know how Allen, Gary et al. had big land etc., well they have a thing for hermitages & I'm going to build one.)

It's so hard for me now, but I'll make it somehow, tho I know I'll never be the same . . .   Your buddy—Lew

[P.S.] This address will reach me for long after I'm gone.

How's Cass? Drum? Diana? Sante Fe? The World? Crud-Critter? Hi!

"Here there is the panic": two Standard Oil Co. tankers had collided just outside the Golden Gate and the resulting oil spill did much damage to bird and shore life, etc.

To Bob Durand, from 52 *Buckelew Street, Marin City,*
26 *January* 1971

Dear Bob,   Thanks for your poem. I once had a friend who went around the world (abt. 1959) and who said everyone he met on the road had got started through either Kerouac or Alan Watts. All those folks with pack-sacks and desert boots. Sigh.

I'd be proud to have my poem in your series.

I SOMETIMES TALK TO KEROUAC
WHEN I DRIVE

Jack?

Yesterday I thought of something
I never had a chance to tell you
and now I don't know what it was

Remember?

176

I'll be in Portland for the month of March. Let's try to get together. Lew

Dear Lew,   good plan.

Ginsberg will be out here at the end of April and will be staying at Kit. at least April 29-May ?. We can agree on the form of your land use then.

As for selecting a site, all that needs be done is (1) selection, (2) informing co-members, and getting their approval, in writing. Once that's done, trees can be chosen & felled (thinning out weak ones etc).

In accord with the general code we've all agreed to, of course, use of automobiles is restricted beyond parking areas except for building and hauling, and once work is done roads are to be returned to nature. Other things—all minor—we can talk @ later and you know it all in yr heart anyhow. I'm away

　　　Feb 14-Mar 2

　　　Mar 7-April 17.　　　So why don't you plan to come up for sure (besides any earlier trips) around May 1 and we'll all confer. Site selection & OK will only take a week and then you can get onto falling. Our water supply, extra and useful tools, storage areas, etc are all available cheerfully to you.

The weather has been dry and warm for a *month* now. wow.

I'm sending a note to Magda—if she's gone on please forward it.

All this sounds so formal. We welcome you to these here woods old friend,   G.

Dear Mom,   Lots of news both good and bad. Thot I could come to tell it to you but just couldn't. I've become such a bad alcoholic I barely function & I didn't want to get drunk and sick at your place like I did on Thanksgiving.

I've got a visitor's permit to work in Portland for the month of

March. I'll be staying with Bill Yardas & hope to use his farm as a drying out place. Then, liquor is hard to get there, so I'll have a better chance.

Magda & I have parted & she is now in Colombia, S.A. having a very exciting adventure. She is seriously thinking of buying land there. We rented the house to Terry Cuddy again. Then Allen Ginsberg gave me his share of the land in Nevada City where Gary has built his house. So the plan is for me to build a cabin there & to really change my life style. No drinking at all is the order. I hope I make it. It's not easy now at all.

Also, building the cabin is a tall order. I have no experience & many fears about that. Can't hire a real carpenter, but maybe can luck out with some help, like Gary did.

So that's the stark news. How are you and the cats?   love,   Lew

To Magda Cregg, from 52 *Buckelew Street, Marin City,*
4 *March* 1971

Got your rapturous letter—sounds like a great beginning. I'll read it to Don Allen tonight. Nothing much going on here. The day after you left Owfee & that yellow dog had a terrible fight. Owfee won (in fact I haven't seen the other dog for a week—maybe it died). Owfee was hurt too—I thought he had a broken leg. For two days he just slept and whimpered and couldn't eat. He's fine now, but still stiff. Some wags planted pot in the Sausalito street planter boxes. Headline pictures etc. Even after they picked them the cops insisted it wasn't real. Now everyone knows where to put their seeds. I'm having a hard time getting myself out of here. Monday I'll hit the road. Write me at Bill's place. Are the stars different? What's the money exchange? Met any good people? We all miss you—it's no fun here at all now. Can't wait to start *my* new life too.   Lewie
[P.S.] Will mail Zig Zags soon

To Magda Cregg, from 606 *Englert Road, Woodland,*
Washington, 11 *April* 1971

Dear Magda—Well it sounds like you're having the expatriate's blues but you used to tell me about how you noticed it in others, so

178

are probably ready to handle them.

It occurs to me that maybe the way to get to the mountains without having to mess with the lowlands would be to go to Barranquilla, then fly to Bogota, then go into the mountains from *above* (or nearly level). Probably you want something about 3 or 4,000 ft (maybe higher down there) and Bogota is about that. Just an idea, since I'm only guessing. But it figures that all passable roads will web out from the city & then you could strike out past them to whatever wilderness.

Also don't be impatient about finding suitable companions right away—there are, after all, only about 40 in the whole world. Most of them are already busy or over the hill.

Another scouting idea is—where are the already functioning coffee and other plantations? There probably are several key areas & they'd have to be fairly accessible. You could bounce in and out of them all & find which general area is prettiest and best. Take the U.S. Even the difference between Oregon & Wash. is very marked— not only physically but politically, socially, & every way. Colombia is so varied maybe a blitz scouting tour would be a ball &, later, a real time-saver.

•

Things at the fun farm are going their muddy way. Rain rain rain rain! The goat had 2 kids April Fool's day. I built a milking stand for her all out of scrap mahogany from the Philippines. It's heavy as a piano. I've been making lots of money & banking it all (I give Nancy $100.00 a month for room & board, can't drink here, & there's nowhere to go). A great hospital, but I couldn't live up here. I've been straight over a month now & some of it is coming back. For one thing I can finally sleep. For another, the appetite is good. And the depression is now only a boredom. Easily beaten by making up little time consuming chores & projects (like the milking stand). You remember the one in Colorado? The goat climbs up on it & her head is held in a pillory and you give her goat candy like oats etc. So she really digs it. Bill's goat is young. Her bag only as big as a softball. We got ½ cup of milk so far. Watery.

I'll pull out of here the 17th (got an extension of my visitor's rights) & will be in SF the 20th April. I'll check on the house & all folks & send gobs of gossip.

•

It's Easter today. Clouds but no rain (yet). Nancy took Caddy & Davey to Portland for an Easter scene with a hippy family. Bill & I at last alone in a quiet house. God I'm glad I never went through total fatherhood. All attention here is fixed at the 3 yr old level—a very dull, exasperating, meaningless place. Davey is really an impossible loud & tiresome brat. I've decided that kids are people you feed for 15 years and then they hate you.

I'm at long last putting my attention toward what makes a car work. The van's cooling system finally had to be replaced entirely ($80.00) and the gears broke again same place you had welded. There's nothing wrong with linkage etc. like everybody always said & I fixed it for only $5.00 welding fee (Chevy garage here wanted $160.00). Found a great old man named Henry who is a super car-wizard having spent his whole life keeping logging equipment running. Now he works on everything for cash (untaxable) to add to his pension. He says to keep Chevy 2 more years and then buy a Toyota pick-up and get a manual & run it for 20 years.

I now have my cabin designed down to the last board (necessary for estimates when building on short money). I can give any lumber yard my bill of materials now & know where I'm at. Have decided I *must* drill my own well first & have enough (I think) to do it.

So April will see [Richard] Werthimer & Ginsberg, and May dig well and build foundation. Cabin in June and July. Then what?

Maybe by then it will all come back & I'll be something like the old Lewie—excited by things and crazy again. Already have actual energy!

I was so much worse than I knew. It must have been awful for you to watch. You were so patient. I really know now where Kerouac was—how the spirit dies so there isn't even fear anymore & the body dies so there isn't any love or courage possible. You can't stop because there isn't anything to stop *with*.

Which leads me to caution you abt. daily coke. It's a very subtle killer, and you've got lots of beautiful things to do.

•

Have definitely decided to have 2 goats (goats need company— they pine away alone). Masa can always milk them when I'm away—or whatever hippies who need the milk—and I'll tether them in all the poison oak patches. Cranky old goat man.

•

180

I suppose this all sounds dull and corny but what I want now is peace. Maybe it's just the body talking, anyway it sounds good right now. It feels like coming out of a horrible and pointless battle. Samsara. All agony & ignorance & nervous highs. Try to help and the poor babies tear you apart for relics. Bah!

I miss you.   love   Lewie

[P.S.] Need anything? Werthimer? Money?

Address, again: April 20 — May 1st or so c/o Tony Dingman & Dant, 1476 Pacific St., San Francisco, Calif. Then c/o Snyder (I'm not going to use Kitkitdizze for address—will think of my own later. Maybe "Welch Gulch"?)

To Lew Welch, from Gary Snyder, Kitkitdizze,
19 April 1971

[. . .] I think the best thing is to set your camp up down near where our last-summer camp was; maybe slightly different spot to give the grass a chance to come back on the old site. You'll need some big pots etc.—and to dig a toilet hole & a garbage pit & you'll be in business. FIRE is the one big danger, and we'll give you some advice on that. The most important danger to impress on everyone.

I'll be gone for all of June, to Japan. Zack [Reisner] will be here, and will be a useful liaison for you regarding any questions or problems; he'll be Fire Marshal and lookout man for the land as a whole. He also has expressed an interest in working for you, if you can pay him a little. Otherwise Steve Sanfield has some carpentry work for Zac.

About a well: The well-digger selects the site for the well (as close as possible to your house site) but if you insist on a location yourself, you forfeit the guarantee, which is "a 3 gallon-per/minute minimum flow well, or no charge for the drilling" at whatever depth they get it—which means likely 120 feet or so; at $9.00 a foot. A well is expensive, you see. Your pump, for a well of that depth, has to be a "force pump" and not a pitcher pump of the sort you suggested. The cylinder in a force pump is down in the bottom of the well. You'll be happy to have as long a handle as you can get on such a pump.

I'll be here up until, roughly, June 1. Expect to hear from you soon as possible; by phone or other means we can arrange meetings with Werthimer & Ginsberg; anytime you arrive for looking things

over and searching out a site you'll be welcome, of course. Oṃ Ah
Huṃ Vajra Guru Padma Siddhi Huṃ   Gary
[On envelope] Chain saws are nice for putting in the winter
firewood (we still don't need one tho)—but I hope you can do your
logging without using one, the trees seem so much happier with 2-
man hand saw

The first part of this letter is lost.

To Lueez and Dan Matthews, from Kitkitdizze, May 1971

Hi Y'all,   I'm definitely depending on you guys now. Sometime
shortly after June 20th. The foreman, Jeff Gold, will be here the
20th and I'll have one other, Zack Reisner, a former Reedy, also.
You 2, and Steve if he can make it (show him this letter) will round
out the crew.

I'll have a comfy camp all set up with everything we need except
for sleeping bags and tools. All food provided. We'll take turns
cooking and cleaning up. Work from 8 to 5 for 5 days a week,
maybe start at 7 in the hot weather w/2 hour siesta. Very orderly
and pleasant.

I feel we'll be all done by July 15th, since Zack and I should have
all materials delivered and the foundations and floor in before you
arrive. After all, it's only a 12 × 20 house.

Already have my gas refrigerator, so we'll have cold drinks in
the heat.

Gary resigned a job in Japan, so will be here for all of June and
July afterwards.

Ginsberg was up. Looks great, and will be a sure visitor this
summer since he plans to stay on in SF for several months.

Please write me right away, as I say I'm definitely depending on
you both, and Steve too. Can he make it? Did he get that grant?

Money very tight, but we'll do her.

My health really fine. I made it. Am on Antabuse now, so have
forced myself to take *no* not any alcohol. You'll see the difference.
love to you all
[P.S.] write real soon

From Welch's carbon copy.

182

To Magda Cregg, from Kitkitdizze, May 1971

Dear Magda, I am here in Kitkitdizze & am trying to get started. I finally went all the way and am on Antabuse. Began May 1st. It really works for me. It puts it into my own hands, automatically, every morning and takes me 48 hours before I can drink, so my mind and energy is all free to go to work. Health very feeble, though. But every day I am stronger.

I realize I was stark raving mad. Am now trying to get back into reality, which is work, doing things, not just sitting around and dreaming and thinking and talking. I didn't realize how helpless I'd become.

I absolutely have to do this to survive. It's hard but it's real, at last, and I know it is the only way for me now.

I'm trying very hard to set up a campsite here to feed the 5 people in my crew. 2 I have on payroll now and am going to need a third one. Both the real carpenters I need to hire worked for Gary last year. My job will be to help keep the camp together and to buy the food and supplies and to help as an apprentice carpenter wherever needed. Will make errands and buy all the lumber.

For the next month Zack and I will make the trails, get estimates on materials and set up a good campsite to feed the crew. Then, after June 15th the carpenters and 3 kids from Reed will join us and the work will really begin, but actually I think we can have the foundations and the floor in by then, too.

I really find it hard to get my head and body rolling, but I am not depressed. I'm just crazy.

I realize I have to learn to do things, to lead people in doing them, to take charge. If I can build this cabin it will be a start. And I really will never drink again.

It seems like I've come a very long ways already but actually I've just been getting the builder together, and he was the hardest part. The stay with Bill in Washington was a great idea, it turns out. I was dry except for wine at dinner for six weeks and eating well and working every day and saving money. My health came back a long way, but actually I didn't really stop drinking. The last week there I was putting away 5 or so drinks before dinner, as a daily thing, and by the time I got back to SF I was in the soup again.

Something snapped in my head & I finally got the point. All my work ahead of me and so many people depending on me, and me an absolute shot old drunk, and totally mad. At Tony's I dried out for the last bad time. I'm sure glad I had his cozy place to do it in. And then I went to Asher Gordon and have been on Antabuse ever since.

It works real well for me. It feels like you're finally putting the thing in your own hands (ironically). You actually put the pill in your own hand every morning & then you can't drink for 2 days, so all that will power nonsense is dispensed with. It is just not possible, that's all. I finally just never think about it. What this does is leave the mind all its energy to getting sane again. And that is the part I've never done before. Before I'd start feeling physically well again (at least no shakes or puking) & I'd feel so good I'd take a little nip. Right back on. Cocteau and Bill Brown both warned me about this, but now I'm actually doing it [it] is hard to explain. Some terrible depressions, then straight days, then absolute bewilderment. But every day it gets clearer. I'm sure it will take several months. Or maybe get to be a daily wonder the rest of my life or something.

It's good to be here where everything is all new anyway. Since it all looks all new, I might as well be doing this. What am I building a cabin for? It is all I think about, that and my new body and new head. There is no future except this cabin & I don't even know how to build! But it's like I was once on acid, there's nothing to it. Nothing. Just details and details and every board put in just right.

I'm going to be a little short of money. I have $3,000 ready and I'll not be able to buy enough food for the crew for the month or 6 weeks it will take. Everything else is covered. I've written Mom to see if she can help, but I doubt it. I'm going to ask Werthimer and Don C. and Richard, too.

I hope this doesn't bug you, but I'm going to ask you, too. Could you loan me $1,000 payback, for sure, before next May. You know I wouldn't ever cheat you & would be super sure to get it back before it would cause you any hardship at all. And without it, all the momentum of having my crew and my material all set & all that energy would just die while I went back to work to earn it. Then all winter with a half house getting ruined.

I've lived in my truck now for 2 weeks and never spend money. Have 3 places to crash in Mill Valley and SF, free. So would finish the house slam-bang, all at once, then shut down, then live in my truck and work every day all winter & could be back in my cabin about the new year's. I know I can do it, I was doing it in Washington the first 6 weeks. I saved just under $1000.

Please do this for me if you think you can. It means so very much to me. And I am really going to do this. And I really need another $1,000. Without it I can't get my second real working and feed everybody. Please help me, honey.

. . . .

You haven't mentioned getting the $200 I sent you in my last letter. It was sent to Santa Marta together with the enclosed bills. It was your share of the return from the income tax and a long letter from me. I sent it sometime after the 20th of April. God I hope it didn't get lost. Should I always register such letters? Yes, I think I will. It was a cashier's check to you written on Wells Fargo, Sausalito. $200 to Maria Magdalena Cregg. In a big brown envelope with Zig Zags.

Do you still always want Zig Zags?

. . . .

I love your letters. Am saving them all for a perfect collection like Burroughs' *Yage Letters*. The honey island story was beautiful and weird. How did the mushrooms start to upset you? Did you ever find yage?

Bogota sounds horrible. How long do the raining seasons last?

I haven't seen Hughie [Cregg] yet, but Jeff looks bigger and bigger. Hard to get anything out of him as you know. I don't think he thinks he could visit you even if he wanted to, or something. And Mav seems to have not done anything with the yard. He and Gabe are moving and Terry [Cuddy] is renting the place for you. Barbara K. wanted it & I told Terry we really don't want people with no money. She's sweet but never could pay. I'll be back in town May 26 to June 1 or 2 and will check in on it for you.

Also you should get Bill Brown or somebody to tear through that yard and cut it back. It's already a jungle.

So many things to tell you. Letters just don't make it. I sure wish we could talk and talk all night like the old days. It's funny, but everybody seems somehow a stranger. Must go to bed now, will mail this before 12 tomorrow.

Please write right away about that check. Maybe we can trace it, or it's insured or something.

And tell me if you can loan me the $1,000. I really miss you sweetie,   Lewie

Dear   I am writing you and the other members of the Bald
Mountain Land Association regarding a small cabin I plan to build
this June. I am building with the permission of Allen Ginsberg to
use a portion of his share of the land.

I would like your approval of the site I have selected.

The site is about 300 feet N.E. of the top of a knoll and is marked
at the position "L" on the attached map. It is on a N.E. slope in a
grove of oaks just at the meeting of the oaks and the pines. The site
is not visible from the parking lot, from Gary's site, nor from the
side, nearer the knoll, which I understand Dick Baker was
considering. Neither is it visible from any of the present trails to
the meadow, or to Gary's site. Gary has already approved of the
site, personally.

I plan a 20 × 12 foot structure to which I'll haul my water, and
which is served by an outside toilet.

Please sign one copy and return it to me if this is agreeable to you.

yours truly,

Yes! I say O.K.!   signed   _____
                          DATE   _____

From Welch's carbon copy.

DAILY LOG
[*From a spiral bound notebook*]

Kitkitdizze   May 14   1971
moved to campsite   began to prepare
crew's kitchen   my bed site   etc.
—write Bruce Boyd cc to Jeff Gold re plans
     "   Werthimer re: $500—Richard?

186

[Dorothy Brownfield, Magda Cregg and Allen Ginsberg all replied that they would loan him the money he had requested. But time had run out for Lew Welch. Gary Snyder found this entry in a journal in Welch's van after his disappearance on 23rd May. It was misdated 22 March 1971.]

I never could make anything work out right and now I'm betraying my friends. I can't make anything out of it—never could. I had great visions but never could bring them together with reality. I used it all up. It's all gone. Don Allen is to be my literary executor—use MSS at Gary's and at Grove Press. I have $2000 in Nevada City Bank of America—use it to cover my affairs and debts. I don't owe Allen G. anything yet nor my Mother. I went Southwest. Goodbye. Lew Welch

INDEXES

A. GENERAL INDEX, INCLUDING RECIPIENTS OF LETTERS

191

Dingman, Tony, II 181, 183–4
Doyle, Kirby, I 148, 207; II 30, 59, 86, 103–4, 116, 121–2
    Letters to: I 201–3, 214–7; II 29, 49, 64–6, 71–7, 81–3, 87–8,
    89–91, 94–6, 106, 113–5, 119
Duerden, Richard, II 88–9, 92
Duncan, Robert, II 5, 7, 51–6, 61, 90, 104, 106, 116, 137, 149
    Letter to: II 51–6
Durand, Bob
    Letter to: II 176–7
Durham, Ed, I 147, II 16

East-West House, I 147, 149, 158; II 26, 30, 47–8, 77
Eigner, Larry, I 210
    Letter to: II 38
Eliot, T. S. I 21, 23, 40, 45, 62, 92, 94, 100, 104–5, 109, 148,
    194, 207, 221; II 24–5, 141, 171–2
Evergreen Review, I 93, 95, 111, 140–1; II 9, 15–6, 19, 23, 25,
    31, 93–4, 120, 123, 127

Ferlinghetti, Lawrence, I 96, 118–9, 123, 148, 160, 176–7, 210;
    II 7, 19, 23, 50, 52, 56–7
Floating Bear, II 77, 82, 86
Foot, II 88–9, 120
Freud, Sigmund, I 48, 52, 83; II 154
Frost, Nemi, I 149; II 104, 116

George, Katharine
    Letters to: II 126–7, 166–9
Ginsberg, Allen, I 93, 96, 101, 103, 109, 123, 145, 149, 160,
    165–6, 170, 182, 206, 208; II 61, 63, 68, 85–6, 99, 104, 116,
    121, 123, 128, 146, 149, 165, 176–8, 180–2, 187. *Howl*, I 96,
    111, 140
    Letters to: I 177–9, 219–23; II 186
Gleason, Ralph, II 127, 136, 138
Gordon, Asher, II 184
Greensfelder, Jean, I 155–6; II 8, 70–71, 77
Griggs, Virginia (Gig), I 10, 24–6, 43, 49–50, 54–5, 58, 77,
    87, 142
Gunther, John, I 22–3

Hadley, Drummond, II 170, 176
Hansen, Bonnie, I 25–6

Harrison, George, II 145
Haselwood, David, I 172, 177, 180, 186, 188–9, 192, 203, 218, 223; II 4, 143, 171
   Letters to: I 181, 198–9, 209–10; II 122
Hatch, Jim, II 47, 170
Hawley, Robert
   Letter to: II 132–3
Heiserman, Jerry, I 147, 156; II 12, 15–9, 22–3
Huncke, Herbert, I 177, 208
Hymes, Del, I 63, 123

i.e., The Cambridge Review, I 85, 91

Janus, I 9
Jones, Dave, I 197
Jones, Frank, I 7–8, 91, 96, 107, 109, 131, 165, 210, 212
Joyce, James, I 32, 105, 109; II 52

Kandel, Lenore, II 22–3, 31–3, 36, 47, 49, 62, 73, 77, 88, 101
Kepecs, Joseph, I 69–70, 77
Kerouac, Jack, I 86, 93, 103, 111, 123, 136, 138, 141, 165, 174, 178, 180, 182–4, 206, 208, 221; II 7–9, 71, 94, 103, 112, 163, 176, 180. *Big Sur*, II 8, 101; *Dharma Bums*, I 158, 191, 194, 197; II 17–8; *Maggie Cassidy*, I 169–70; "October in the Railroad Earth," II 129; *On the Road*, I 103–4, 126–7, 133, 135, 186; II 7; *The Subterraneans*, I 134–6
   Letters to: I 167–72, 175–7, 184–6, 189–92, 199–201, 217–9; II 18–9, 22–4, 101–2, 117–8
Kline, Franz, I 144
Koller, Jim, II 170
   Letter to: II 175–6
Körte, Mary Norbert
   Letter to: II 148–50
Kyger, Joanne, I 148, 156, 164, 183, 186, 192, 194; II 7, 26, 47–8, 59, 71–2, 96, 98, 103–4, 107, 125, 162
   Letters to: I 149, 173–5; II 30–1, 34–5, 47–8, 61–3, 78, 116–7

Lamantia, Philip, I 148, 209; II 104, 116
LaVigne, Bob, I 142, 145, 149, 199, 209
Lawrence, D. H., I 184, 187; II 60
Leong, Charlie, I 82, 84, 104, 128
Linenthal, Mark, I 164; II 136

Loewinsohn, Ron, II 112–3

Mathews, Lueez and Dan
    Letter to: II 182
McClure, Michael, I 147, 151, 153, 177, 186, 188, 198, 203, 206,
    210, 213; II 10, 16, 28–30, 71, 77, 104, 112, 116, 120, 171
McCorkle, Locke, I 153, 163
McDarrah, Fred, II 124, 170
Meltzer, David, II 104, 107, 132–3, 171
    Letter to: II 170–1
Meyer, Lawrence, II 74–6, 79–82, 105–6
Miller, Henry, I 23, 64, 111
Mills, Barriss, I 112, 121–2
Montgomery Ward & Co., I 74–5, 77, 100, 115–6, 118, 124, 137
Moore, Marianne, I 216–8, 223; II 85, 112
    Letters from: II 106, 110, 115, 134
Much Ado About Nothing, I 14
Muir, John, I 124, 195

Nessel, Jack, II 128
New American Poetry, The, I 189, 198, 201, 206–8, 216–7; II 85,
    106, 123, 151
New Writing in the U.S.A., The, II 129, 151
New Yorker, I 77, 89–91, 136; II 21, 107
Nomad, II 123
Novak, Pete and Sally, II 63–6, 90

O'Brien, Joseph
    Letter to: II 160
Olson, Charles, I 93, 146, 186, 197, 206, 208–9; II 6, 38, 61, 71,
    121. *Apollonius of Tyana*, I 198; *Maximus Poems* II 56–7, 106;
    "Projective Verse," II 10
    Letters to: II 4–5, 56–7, 67
Origin, II 47
Orlovsky, Peter, I 145; II 99
Oser, Peter, I 57–8, 152

Patchen, Kenneth, I 115–6, 120; II 85, 165
Petersen, Will
    Letter to: II 9
Po Chu-i, II 90–91

Poetry, See Rago, Henry
Pound, Ezra, I 35, 59, 62, 101, 105, 109, 131, 140, 206–7, 214, 221; II 106, 124

Rago, Henry
  Letters to: II 123–5, 127–8
Reisner, Zack, II 181–3
Rexroth, Kenneth, I 106, 114, 117–8, 121, 128, 135, 137–8, 140, 163, 194, 197, 209, 221; II 139
Reynolds, Lloyd, II 16, 143
Richardson, Elizabeth
  Letter to: II 164–5
Rilke, Rainer Maria, II 106–7, 111, 125
Rimbaud, Arthur, I 103, 105; II 22, 53, 56
Rumaker, Michael, I 208

Saijo, Albert, I 149, 156, 158–9, 163–5, 167–71, 187–8, 193, 200, 206, 213, 219; II 6–7, 30, 48, 77, 82, 87, 92, 161
Sales, Grover, I 81, 83, 85, 92, 94, 104, 115–8, 121, 125, 133, 135; II 141–3, 164–5. "One-Man Plays," II 141–2
Sales, Tommy, I 81, 83, 85, 92, 104, 115–9, 123–4, 131–2; II 108
San Francisco Chronicle, I 136; II 107, 127, 135–6, 156–8
San Francisco Review, I 157, 161; II 123
San Francisco State College Poetry Center, I 153–4, 161, 164; II 135–8
Schevill, James
  Letter to: II 135–40
Shekkeloff, Brian and Mertis, I 149, 206, 215
Sh'n and Yee, I 32, 39, 61, 128
Shoemaker, Jack, II 151
  Letter to: II 142–3, 173–4
Smith, Elspeth
  Letters to: II 147–8, 151–4
Snyder, Gary, I 1, 4, 6, 85–6, 91, 93, 105, 107, 115, 119, 132, 137–42, 144, 146–51, 153–4, 156, 161, 166, 169, 173, 176, 186, 191, 197, 206, 208, 210, 212; II 4, 18, 59, 61, 85–7, 94, 105, 107, 125, 127–8, 149, 161, 164, 176, 178, 181–3, 187. "Berry Feast" II 111; *Earth House Hold* II 159; *Myths & Texts* I 121, 123–5, 186, 197–8; "Night Highway Ninety-Nine" II 17, 36, 47–8; *Riprap* I 181, 183; "Xrist" II 36
  Letters from: I 101–2, 112–4; II 67–8, 143–4, 146, 174, 177, 181–2

196

B. INDEX OF WORKS BY LEW WELCH